Southwestern Country Classics

Southwestern Country Classics

Early American Woodworking Projects

Gloria Saberin

TAB TAB BOOKS
Blue Ridge Summit, PA

FIRST EDITION
FIRST PRINTING

©1993 by **TAB Books**.
TAB Books is a division of McGraw-Hill, Inc.

Library of Congress Cataloging-in-Publication Data

Saberin, Gloria.
    Southwestern country classics : early American woodworking
projects / by Gloria Saberin.
        p.   cm
    Includes index.
    ISBN 0-8306-4195-5 (pbk.)
    1. Woodwork. 2. Woodwork—Southwest, New.   I. Title
TT180.S325   1992
684′08—dc20   92-23367
                                                                  CIP

Acquisitions editor: Stacy V. Pomeroy
Editorial team: Joanne M. Slike, Executive Editor
                Terry Belanger, Editor
                Kristine D. Lively-Helman, Indexer
Production team: Katherine G. Brown, Director
                Wanda S. Ditch, Layout
                Ollie Harmon, Typesetting
                Susan E. Hansford, Typesetting
                Tara Ernst, Proofreading
Design team: Jaclyn J. Boone, Designer
            Brian Allison, Associate Designer
Cover design: Lori E. Schlosser
Cover illustration: Douglas Robson   HT1

Credits

Special thanks for the use of photographs to El Rancho de las Golondrinas, Santa Fe, New Mexico; Kit Carson Museums, Taos, New Mexico; and Vaughan C. Chambers, Wilmington, Delaware Illustrations and all other photographs by Paul C. Saberin, Chambersburg, Pennsylvania

Acknowledgments

My decision to write *Southwestern Country Classics* was spontaneous. Many people helped me to complete all aspects of the book within the allotted time frame. The staffs of museums and antique shops in the Southwest allowed me to measure, sketch, and photograph items in which I was particularly interested. I am especially grateful to Neil Poese, director of the Kit Carson Museums in Taos, and Louann C. Jordan, curator of programs and publicity for El Rancho de las Golondrinas in Santa Fe, for their interest, encouragement, and expertise. Their respective museums, both located on the Camino Real, are wonderful sources for research into the traditions, culture, and lives of the early settlers of the Southwest.

Special thanks also go to my cousin, Vaughan Chambers, who crafted the table, chest, and padre chair for me. A fine woodworker, Vaughan also helped critique my other work.

The heart-shaped decorative clasp for the bride's chest was made by my teenage friend, Dan Parkolay.

Finally, I am grateful to Bonnie Brechbill for her assistance, and to my patient husband, Paul Saberin, whose fine drawings and plans illustrate and enhance the book.

Small household accessories

Furniture

DURING A RECENT painting trip to the Southwest, I was thrilled by the region's unusual and colorful antiques. I could barely wait to return to my workshop and make some reproductions for my own use. In this book, I am including many of my favorites so that you too may enjoy making them.

The blending of Spanish and Indian motifs and methods is evident in these antiques from the sixteenth, seventeenth, and eighteenth centuries. Hundreds of rugged miles from the nearest urban centers in Mexico, the early settlers used only the materials at hand to create designs that evolved into the unique style of the Southwest. The antiques adapted for this book are representative of furniture and household accessories found in the haciendas and simple homes of the earliest settlers.

I have selected a wide variety of pieces so that you will be able to make many of the projects, regardless of your woodworking experience. If you are relatively inexperienced, start with a few good, basic hand tools and make a sconce or chandelier. Add more tools as you need them, and then try more complex projects. Gradually, you can build a Southwestern "Country Classics" collection of your own.

As your collection grows, I hope your interest in learning more about the history, culture, and traditions of this fascinating region will also grow.

SOUTHWESTERN furniture was the first truly Early American style to emerge in what is now the United States. This is a surprising, perhaps even shocking, revelation to those of us who have grown up "knowing" that Early American meant only the cherry, maple, and pine furniture crafted by artisans in the original thirteen colonies.

We need to look more carefully into the history of our Southwestern states. A large number of well-established Native American towns, called *pueblos*, dotted the landscape even before Columbus landed in the islands of the Caribbean. Many of the pueblos had populations of thousands and a culture that included architecture, pottery, and rug making. During the late sixteenth century, the Spanish pushed exploration and settlement into what is now Texas, New Mexico, and Arizona in their zealous search for gold, treasure, and converts to Christianity.

By the time the Pilgrims landed on Plymouth Rock, ranchers, soldiers, and friars had been long settled in small communities throughout Texas and New Mexico. In 1609 the Spanish established a capital in Santa Fe. The complex of buildings known as the Palace of Governors, has been in continuous use ever since, and has a fascinating history of its own. It is now a major museum for New Mexican history and culture. By 1630 Santa Fe had a population of over a thousand soldiers, Franciscans, and civilians, and at least a thousand ranchers were established along the Rio Grande. The only contact with the civilized urban centers far to the south was the trail known as *El Camino Real*, or The Royal Road. Begun in 1598, the route extended twelve hundred hazardous miles from Mexico City to Santa Fe and wound through rough terrain, desert, mountains, and Indian territory.

Caravans plodding north and south traveled this route for hundreds of years. They stopped at established stations called *parajes* in order to replenish their supplies of water, grass, and firewood. Most caravans consisted of farmers, artisans, militia, livestock, and the ever-present religious. Even so, settlements in the far north often had to wait three or four years between caravans for supplies and reinforcements.

This isolation forced the Spanish homesteaders to become very self-reliant. Unlike the English and northern European colonists of the eastern coastal states, the Spanish readily adapted Indian methods, designs, and materials when they proved to be beneficial. The adobe style of building used in the large pueblos was quickly adopted by the new arrivals. The thick walls of adobe clay cooled the interior in the heat of the day and retained the heat of the sun for the cool nights. In addition, there was an abundance of materials for construction. Even today the architectural style of Santa Fe and environs is overwhelmingly adobe or simulated adobe.

In their former homes, the early Spanish settlers of all classes had been accustomed to ornately carved Spanish-Moorish furniture with metal decorative features. This style was impossible to duplicate in their new surroundings. The settlers had no hardwoods or metals to use for their household items, nor were their tools adequate if they could have found such materials. Using local softwoods and simple hand tools, they blended simplified Spanish and Moorish patterns with the designs, motifs, and methods of the Pueblo Indians to fashion their necessities. In crafting their furniture and accessories for home, farm, and church, the artisans of the early Southwest developed a style unique to that region.

The style of the Southwest is simple, functional, decorative, and elegant. The decorations are an integral part of the whole. Simple chip-and-incision carving enhances and lightens the overall design but never hampers its function. The early methods of joining, so well suited to the climate and woods available to these artisans, are special features of this style. The durability and attractiveness of these early antiques have made them treasured items in homes and museums of the Southwest throughout the centuries.

The introduction of rail transport in the late 1800s brought factory-made furniture from the east. Its temporary popularity in the late nineteenth century replaced the production of handmade traditional furniture in the urban centers for a period of years.

Fortunately, through efforts spearheaded by the Spanish Colonial Arts Society and aided by state and private commissions, old traditional designs, patterns, and methods of producing furniture were researched and published during the 1920s. Indigenous furniture construction and craft-making were revived and encouraged by the government of New Mexico. Since then, the popularity and appreciation of the authentic style of the Southwest have increased throughout the entire country. This style is now recognized as a major artistic contribution that is unique to the United States. If you make any of the projects in this book, you will find that the elegant, simple design adds a decorative accent to your other antiques and reproductions.

THE PROJECTS IN this book are reproductions and adaptations of antique furniture and accessories that I found on a recent stay in the Southwest. The original pieces were made during the seventeenth through nineteenth centuries by colonists who were mainly of Hispanic background. The Spanish influence is quite evident in most of the projects. Others show Indian origins or a creative blend of the two cultures.

The earliest settlers in this region included many experienced craftsmen. Their work, however, was greatly restricted by the lack of hardwood and metals.

A distinctive feature of Southwestern antiques is the use of simple joinery without benefit of nails, screws, or glue. Boards were pinned together with square pegs set at opposing angles. Joints were made with through-mortise-and-tenon, which made it possible to wedge the tenons if the joints should loosen. In the Southwest, each 24-hour period has a great fluctuation of temperature. Wood joints tend to work loose easily under these conditions. Some joints, such as those on chairs and settees, were also pinned through the tenons to give added stability.

For the projects in this book, I use methods of joining like those found in the early furniture. If you prefer to use nails or screws in your work, be careful to adjust the patterns accordingly. I suggest you sink any hardware and cover with plugs to maintain an authentic appearance.

Some of the photographs show the original antiques in their present setting. Other photos are of my reproductions. In some instances, I adapt the construction to make a project sturdier or easier to make.

One charming aspect of the antiques pictured throughout the book is the lack of precision in carving and painting the decorative elements within a piece. If you look carefully, you will see that each section in the back of a settee, for instance, differs a little from the others. Where there are scallops (painted or carved), they are slightly irregular. Knots were often left in wood unless they occurred near an edge or joint where they would weaken the item. When you are making a project, keep a creative approach to the purely decorative elements and your result will be as attractive and charming as the original.

Patterns

I provide plans for curving areas wherever possible. The curved sections are gridded so that you can enlarge them more precisely. In these cases, I indicate the size to which the grid squares must be enlarged before a pattern is transferred to the wood stock. The method I use is to lay out a grid of desired size on a large sheet of paper. Number and grid the coordinates on both the small grid in the book and the larger grid. Then, transfer the coordinate points to the large grid. Next, using a French curve, connect the points. Check the configuration several times as you proceed.

An easy way to enlarge plans is to use an enlarging copier at a commercial printer or copy center. Copy the pattern at book size first, and then enlarge the pattern until the grid squares are the required size for a full-sized pattern. I like this method because I can make several copies to use later after I have the pattern at full size. For very large pieces, you might have to cut and paste together several sheets of the enlarged copy.

A pattern can be transferred to the wood with the use of carbon paper. Instead of using carbon paper, I often rub a soft pencil on the back of the pattern and then trace. Another method is to cut a template of cardboard from the pattern and trace around it to transfer the design to the wood stock. This works well when you need to fit several pieces on the board around knotholes and other imperfections. One of my octogenarian friends, Harry Davis, always glues the paper pattern directly to the wood and cuts through paper and wood at the same time. This solution is perfect for the intricate patterns he cuts.

Wood

When the first settlers arrived in the Southwest, they found much the same variety of trees as exist there today. The mountains had ponderosa pine, Douglas fir, and some aspens and tall pines. In most sections, however, such pines as the Jeffrey, pine nut, lodgepole, and juniper, in addition to the cottonwood along the rivers, constituted the major wood sources. Trees in the more arid regions were merely large shrubs, so obtaining enough wood for furniture was a constant challenge.

With today's lumberyards, this aspect of your project should be simple. Although they were not available for use by the craftsmen of the early Southwest, teak and Honduras mahogany are excellent woods to use for many of the large projects in this book. These woods are durable, do not crack or split, and weather to a lovely soft gray typical of the antiques of the Southwest. No protective finish is needed for pieces crafted of teak or mahogany. I list pine as the wood of choice in most of the projects because it was used for the original, but the life of the piece may be extended by using mahogany or teak.

If you desire to make your projects of pine, as the settlers did, go to a good lumberyard and get well-seasoned, clear pine (ponderosa, if available). Poplar is also a possible choice for legs and arms of large pieces. I selected basswood for the carreta and cheeseboard because it is light; has a very fine, even grain; and is easy to carve.

It is important to pick out the wood yourself in order to get straight pieces with as few blemishes as possible. A local mill planes my wood to the proper thickness and allows me to examine each piece. This costs a bit more but saves much time and difficulty later on.

My materials lists give the exact measurements for the finished pieces. (Do allow extra length for tenons, which are trimmed flush after assembly.) If a 1-inch board is listed, it means a 1-inch finished measurement. Wood is cut thinner today than in colonial days, so occasionally you might require wood that is custom milled for a project.

When the project requires a large width of wood for a tabletop or side of a chest, join together several pieces of stock by gluing, doweling, or biscuiting edge to edge. If you are doing this yourself, you need large furrnniture pipe clamps and a method of planing the edges perfectly straight. Alternate the direction of the end curve in adjacent boards in order to lessen the chance of the finished piece twisting and curving out of shape after you finish the project.

The projects in this book can be made without a wood shop or complicated power tools. Sometimes I make a small project or the decoration, chips, or incising of a larger one while sitting outside or working on a tray by the fireside. People often tell me they would like to make things of wood but feel they need a complete workshop before they can start. All you really need is space, good ventilation, and a sturdy bench or table in order to begin.

If you are just getting started at woodworking, buy some of the basic tools and add others when needed. I suggest starting with hand tools and an electric drill. My initial tool kit included the following:

- crosscut saw
  (10 teeth to the inch)
- coping saw
- keyhole saw
- 16-ounce claw hammer
- tack hammer
- wooden mallet
- pliers—regular and
  needle nose
- set of screwdrivers—
  regular and Phillips
- set of chisels
- eggbeater drill
- rasps and files—
  straight and curved

- nail set
- brace and bits
- doweling centers
- marking gauge
- awl
- jack plane
- metal measuring tape
- carpenter's square
- plumb line
- level
- metal bench rule
- utility knife
- X-Acto knife set and blades
- clamps
- woodworking vise

Buy the best tools possible and keep them sharp and the handles tight.

Over the years I have added some simple power tools and now have a table saw, a band saw, a scroll saw, a drill press, a router, two belt sanders, and a palm sander.

My power tools are mounted on portable worktables so that I can move them around in the shop and even outside when the weather permits. It is fun to work outdoors, especially when sanding or cutting large amounts of wood. I enjoy woodworking in the fresh air, and I hope you will try it. If you move power tools outside, be certain to use heavy-duty extension cords and arrange them so you will not trip over them.

Power tools require less strength on your part and make the work go much faster. Add these tools when you feel you really need them. If you would use a power tool only occasionally, it might be more prudent to borrow it or to have another craftsman make that special section for you. When I need turning done, I often take the wood to a local woodworker who is an expert at the lathe. Because of the difficulty in finding beautiful, large wood suitable for turning, it is sensible to have it cut by a master turner instead of taking the chance of ruining the piece by turning it myself.

After purchasing power tools, do not operate them until you know how to do so correctly and safely. Be certain they are mounted securely on their stands and have safe electrical hookups.

Power tools are a helpful option in woodworking. If you are planning to make several of one item, they are almost essential.

The use of power tools does not detract from the appearance of reproductions as long as the finishing is done by hand. I prefer to do dovetailing and mortising by hand as I like the work, and the irregularity of the handwork adds to the charm of the completed piece. Adapt these patterns to suit yourself. Whether you wish to follow the early craftsmen in actual methods of production or to use the most modern tools available, you will enjoy the projects in this book. All were originally made long ago by people who took pride in their creativity.

Safety

Safety is an important consideration when working with any kind of sharp implement, especially in woodworking. With a few precautions, you can make woodworking as safe as any daily household task. Nine basic guidelines are important features of any workshop:

1. Keep the floor clear of all debris.
2. Keep the floor dry to prevent shocks or slipping.

3. Do not wear loose, floppy clothing that can catch in tools.
4. Keep your hair pulled back securely if it is long.
5. Wear safety glasses or a face shield.
6. Keep your tools sharp and the handles tight.
7. Unplug all power tools when not working with them or when changing blades or servicing them in any way.
8. Do not operate a power tool unless you know how to use it properly.
9. If an extension cord is necessary, use a heavy-duty cord with three prongs.

Decorating & finishing

Many of the early Southwestern pieces of furniture were originally left without a finishing coat of paint or varnish, and they have weathered to a soft, grayish tan. This is especially true of carved and incised furniture, which was almost never painted. Because new wood looks garish when first worked, I paint on a gray or brown stain, wipe down the wood with a soft cloth, and sometimes add a protective coat of matte-finish polyurethane. I do not use any finish on mahogany or teak.

The major decoration in the Southwest consisted of roughly executed carving and painting. Typical designs were the simple geometric patterns that evolved from a melding of Spanish, Moorish, and Native Indian motifs.

Carving was usually chip carving, consisting of different-sized notches repeated in several sequences to make a distinct pattern in the wood. Other sections of the same piece often had parallel incisions cut in the wood to create a design. The rails along a chair front were usually incised, but the edges of shelves were more often chipped. Carving was never done where it would interfere with the function of the piece; for example, carving is never found on the seat or arms of a chair or on the top of a chest, which might be used for sitting.

The painted decorations were often geometric, although simple animal forms were sometimes depicted in more complicated, illustrative designs.

Paint was made from egg or animal glue mixed with locally produced pigments, and it was very durable. Colors on the frontier were limited to the yellow ochres, reds, and browns made from iron oxides; gray and black derived from charcoal; white made from gypsum; and blues and greens obtained from vegetable matter. Even today, this palette of strong earth colors is a distinguishing feature of the Southwestern style.

When finishing your reproduction, be sure you sand the edges until they are rounded. Even those shown in the plans as straight or angled should be gently rounded, which gives a more pleasing and authentic appearance to the finished product.

This book includes patterns for the decoration of each project and a selection of colors that are suitable. Of course, you can modify the colors to match your own color scheme. By keeping to the general Southwestern palette, however, you will produce a more authentic and acceptable adaptation.

Small Household Accessories

Through a careful selection of small accessories, the frontier woman turned a house into a home. These artistic choices were a reflection of each family's character and gave a distinctive look to the sparsely furnished homes of the Southwest. As Hispanic colonists traveled north to their first homes in the "new west," they may have carried treasured heirlooms with them, but they were usually small and few in number.

The rest of their household items were fashioned by family members from materials available at the new homesite. Early homemakers decorated their small homes as best they could with the limited resources available. Over time, they created a new style that blended the Hispanic-Moorish tradition of their homelands with Native Indian motifs and patterns.

During the early seventeeth century, Hispanic colonists started to weave rugs and cloth from the wool of their sheep. Local dyes and design motifs made these items distinctive. Many colonists established family and business dynasties, some of which flourish even today in the Southwest, often in their original locations.

The production of blankets, coverlets, and rugs started cottage industries. The woven items were used in the family's own home and were also sold to other settlers. The early housewives hung these colorful woolens as decorations for their plain adobe walls, doorways, and windows and folded them to cover wooden seats.

Even such simple wooden accessories as sconces and shelves were decorated with carved or painted motifs. Little by little, these colorful touches brightened up the dark interiors of the plain adobe homes.

The small pieces presented in the first part of this book are representative of the functional, decorative accessories chosen for their homes by the early Hispanic-American settlers.

Sconce
(candelero)

SCONCES WERE COMMON household accessories in the early homes of the Southwest. Called *candeleros* in Spanish, they were sometimes painted or incised with a pattern to make them more decorative, but their primary purpose was functional. They were easily carried from room to room and hung on pegs in the wall so that candlelight was available wherever needed. Because candles were scarce, the sconces often were carried around rather than placed in every room.

The original of this project is in a Taos museum. The simple geometric shape (Figs. 1-1 and 1-2) and colorful painted design make this piece particularly attractive. It was crudely made but artistically designed and painted.

I used pine for this project. After assembling the sconce, I sanded the edges to round them slightly. This was usually done by the early craftsman to prevent the corners of the soft wood from splintering.

The design was incised in the wood before painting. I used a woodburning tool to outline the design and then painted it with acrylic craft paint. When it was dry, I spread medium-brown stain over the entire surface and rubbed it off briskly with a soft cloth. This process resulted in the soft, aged look of the original sconce.

4 Small household accessories

Part	Number Required	Size (inches)
A (back)	1	¾ × 5½ × 14⅜
B* (shelf)	1	¾ × 4¼ × 4¾
C* (brace)	1	¾ × 2⁷⁄₁₆ × 3⅜

*For B and C, allow an extra ¼ inch in length for tenons; trim off flush after assembly
Note: Measurements given are finished dimensions.

Miscellaneous:

- Wooden dowels or pegs for fastening
- Glue, if desired
- Woodburning tool; white and red acrylic paint.

1. Cut out A, B, and C. See Fig. 1-3. Allow ¼ inch in length for tenons on B and C.
2. Drill hole for candle.
3. Cut mortise in A and drill holes for pegs. Enlarge mortise until tenons on C and B fit tightly into A.
4. Wedge, if necessary.
5. Sand.
6. Burn designs on A with woodburner.
7. Paint according to pattern (Fig. 1-4) and rub off paint a little for a rustic appearance.
8. Sand corners slightly to give a well-worn look.

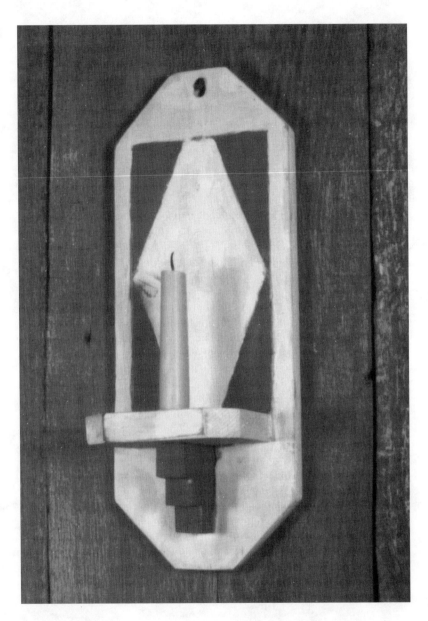

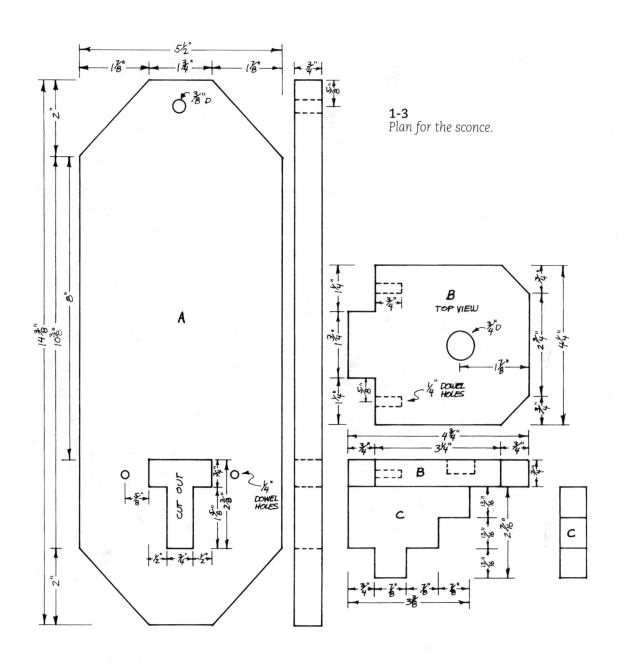

1-3
Plan for the sconce.

Sconce (candelero) 7

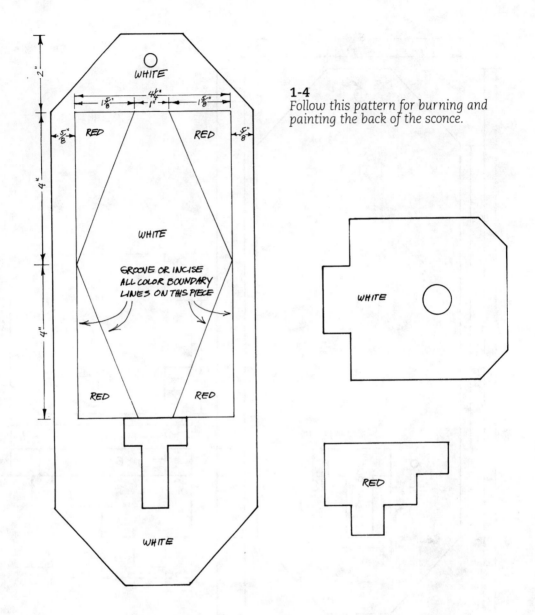

1-4
Follow this pattern for burning and painting the back of the sconce.

WHITE

RED   RED

WHITE

GROOVE OR INCISE
ALL COLOR BOUNDARY
LINES ON THIS PIECE

RED   RED

WHITE

2"

4"

4"

1⅝"   4¼"   1⅝"
          1"

⅝"   ⅝"

WHITE

RED

8 Small household accessories

Chandelier (arania)

THIS CHANDELIER is a typical early Southwestern light fixture. I saw many versions in the Southwest; some had two arms and some four. The original chandelier from which I derived this pattern hangs in a display room in a popular Taos museum.

The arms can have a chipped design, as well as a red-and-blue painted design. The remainder of the assembly is unpainted. See Fig. 2-1.

This general style of wooden candelabra can be raised and lowered by means of a rope passed through a pulley on the ceiling and fastened to a cleat on the wall. This extremely practical design was popular throughout the early western colonies (Fig. 2-2). It possibly reflects an early artisan's attempt to replicate in wood a more elaborate Spanish metal light fixture.

Because it has holes for twelve candles, the original of this project was probably made for a large room. Whatever its origin, this functional, attractive light can be used with almost any style of country furnishings.

Use poplar, pine, or any other type of desired wood for this project.

Materials list

Part	Number Required	Size (inches)
A and B (arm)	2	1½ × 1½ × 18
C (vertical stem)	1	1¼ round × 18½
Small dowel	1	¼ × 2

Note: Measurements given are finished dimensions.

Miscellaneous:
- Sandpaper
- Paints—red and teal blue craft paint, if desired
- Rope—about 10 feet of ¼-inch-thick rope.

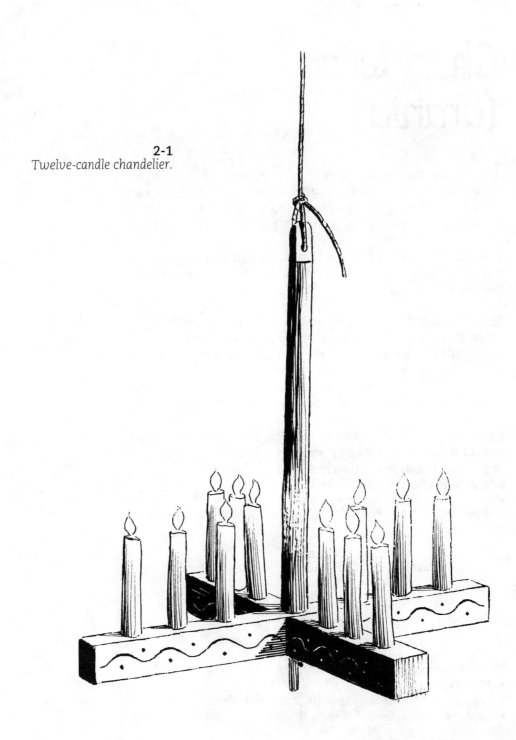

2-1
Twelve-candle chandelier.

10 Small household accessories

A reproduction chandelier.

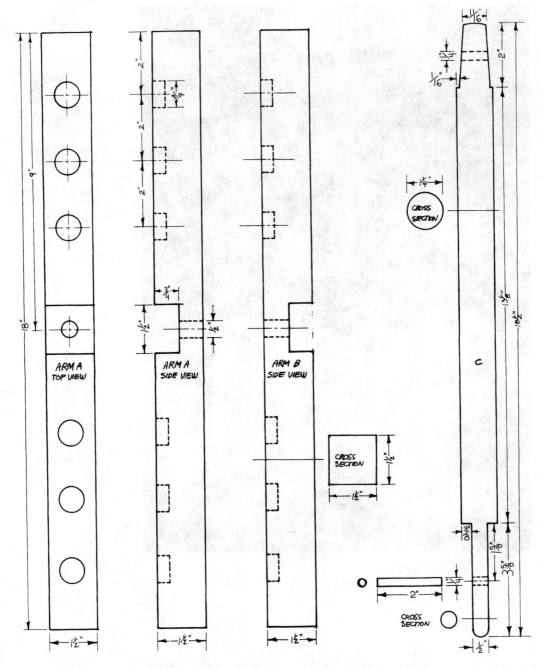

2-3 Plan for the arms (A and B) and the stem (C)

12 Small household accessories

1. Cut out arms A and B as in Fig. 2-3 and drill holes as indicated. Sand.
2. Cut out vertical stem C and shape at both ends (Fig. 2-3). Sand.
3. Drill holes.
4. Decorate as desired with paint or chipped design. See patterns in Fig. 2-4.
5. Assemble and add rope as in Fig. 2-5. Note detail in Fig. 2-6.

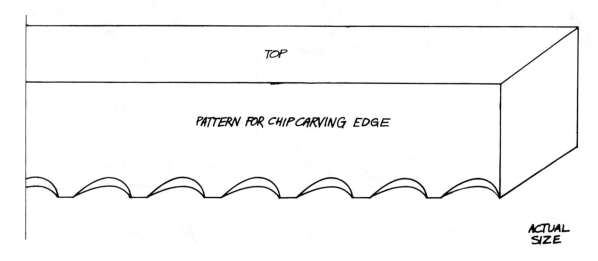

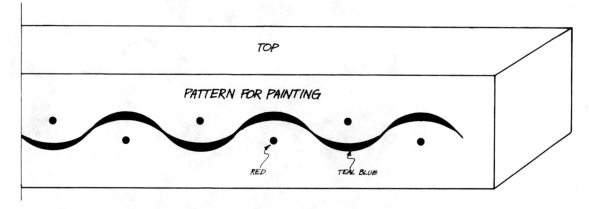

2-4 *Choose one of these patterns for decorating your chandelier.*

Chandelier (arania) 13

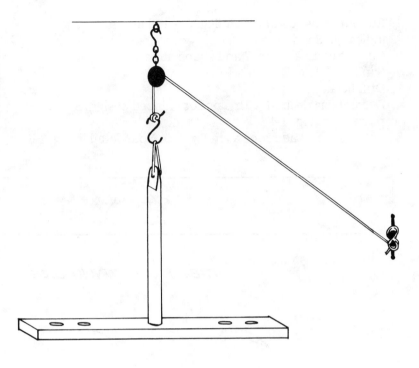

2-5
*The chandelier is hung
from the ceiling in
this manner.*

2-6
*Underside of the
reproduction shows
the dowel that holds the
chandelier together.*

14 Small household accessories

Display shelf (alazen)

SMALL MOVABLE SHELVES, similar to the shelf shown in Figs. 3-1 and 3-2, were common fixtures in the early settlers' homes. They sometimes held small religious figures called *Santos*. Santos depicted the holy virgin or a saint. They were made of wood, covered with a gypsum mixture, and then painted in bright colors. Many of the Santos were made by itinerant craftsmen called *Santeros* who traveled from one settlement to another during the late seventeenth and early eighteenth centuries.

These shelves with their images were used as small home shrines or altars. Often, candles were placed near them as prayer offerings or as thanks for blessings. A large hacienda could set aside a small room for use as a chapel, but the average home made do with a little display shelf.

The original of this shelf was stained red, so I painted my reproduction the same color, and sanded the corners afterward to give it a used appearance.

The simple pattern of the shelf is very appealing and easy to construct. Make one for yourself and another for a friend. Displaying a favorite decorative item, the shelf would be equally at home in a living room, den, or kitchen.

Use pine or poplar for this project.

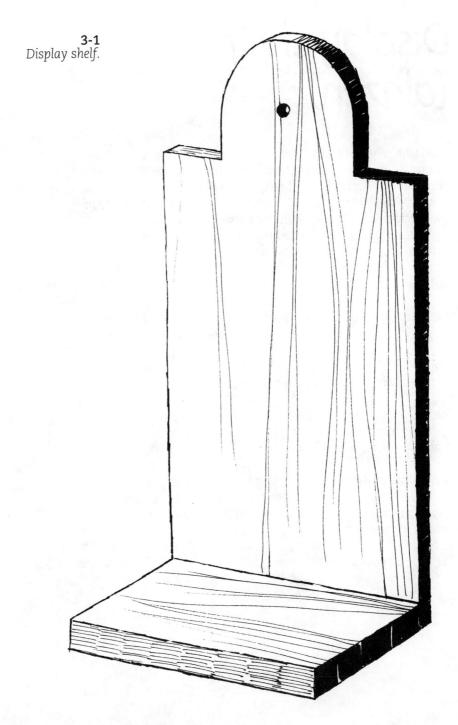

16 Small household accessories

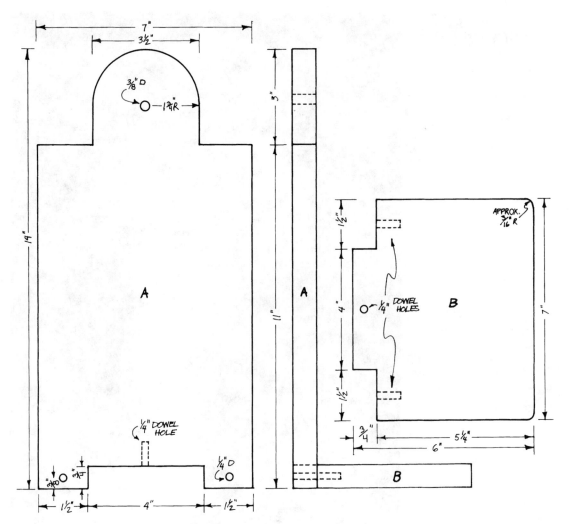

3-2 *Plan for cutting out the shelf.*

Display shelf (alazen) 17

18 Small household accessories

Part	Number Required	Size (inches)
Back	1	¾ × 7 × 19
Shelf	1	¾ × 6 × 7

Note: Measurements given are finished dimensions.

Miscellaneous
- ¼-inch doweling or pegs
- Glue
- Red paint or stain

1. Cut out A and B and sand well. See Fig. 3-3.
2. Drill holes for pinning or hanging.
3. Insert pins and glue or wedge, if necessary. See Fig. 3-4.
4. Sand again.
5. Stain with red paint or stain.

Construction tips

3-4
Photo shows how the shelf is joined and pinned.

Trunk stands

A SPANISH TRADITION brought by the early colonists to the New World was that of placing trunks and chests on stands to keep them above the ground. The stands varied from 6 inches to 2 feet high. They were especially practical in the climate of the Southwest. Damp floors resulted from extensive diurnal temperature changes and the lack of basements in adobe buildings. The small chests were usually made from rather thin wood and undoubtedly lasted much longer when kept above the floor.

The principal differences between the Spanish trunk stands and those made in the New World were in size and decoration. The latter were simple racks of wood, whereas the Spanish stands were often massive and as elaborately carved or painted as the trunks they supported. I seldom saw two sets of stands with the same design, but every chest was sitting on a stand of some kind.

This chapter provides patterns for three styles of trunk stands. Figures 4-1 and 4-2 illustrate two of these. The three patterns vary in size and complexity, so choose one that best suits your needs. The originals were unpainted, but the stands can be painted and decorated if you wish.

Use pine or another wood of your choice for this project.

Materials List

Stand 1 (Fig. 4-3)

Part	Number Required	Size (inches)
Braces	2	½ × 2 × 21½
Legs	4	1½ × 3½ × 6

Stand 2 (Fig. 4-4)

Part	Number Required	Size (inches)
Front Keys (A)	2	¾ × 5½ × 24
Back legs (B)	2	¾ × 5½ × 12
Braces (C)	2	½ × 2½ × 23½

Stand 3 (Fig. 4-5)

Part	Number Required	Size (inches)
Legs	4	¾ × 3½ × 14

Note: Measurements given are finished dimensions.

Miscellaneous:
- 4 pieces, ⅝-inch doweling of desired length for braces
- 2 pieces, 1-inch doweling of desired length for braces

1. To determine length of braces, measure depth of trunk for which you will use stand (see Fig. 4-6) and add the following to depth of trunk for each type of stand:

Stand 1	5 inches
Stand 2	5 inches
Stand 3	1¾ inches

If you are not making the stand for a specific trunk, use all measurements as given in the desired plan.
2. Cut out legs and sand.
3. Cut out braces and sand.
4. Assemble without glue; wedge, if necessary, to make stable.

Construction tips for all patterns

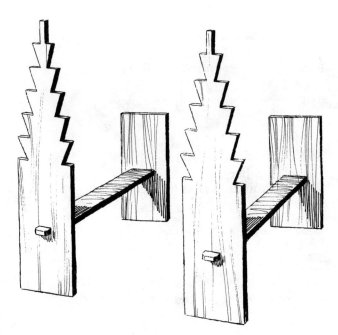

4-1
Trunk stands.

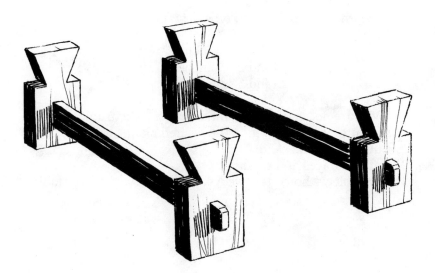

22 Small household accessories

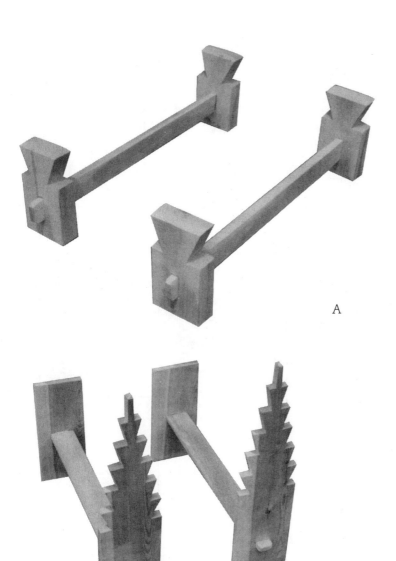

A

4-2
*Reproduction stands style
1(A) and style 2(B).*

B

Trunk stands 23

4-3
Plan for style 1 stand.

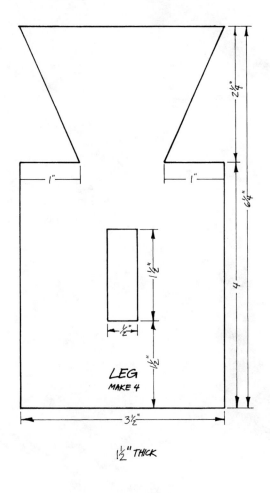

LEG
MAKE 4

1½" THICK

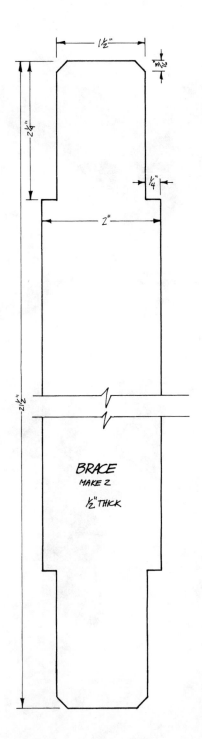

BRACE
MAKE 2
½" THICK

24 Small household accessories

4-4 *Plan for style 2 stand.*

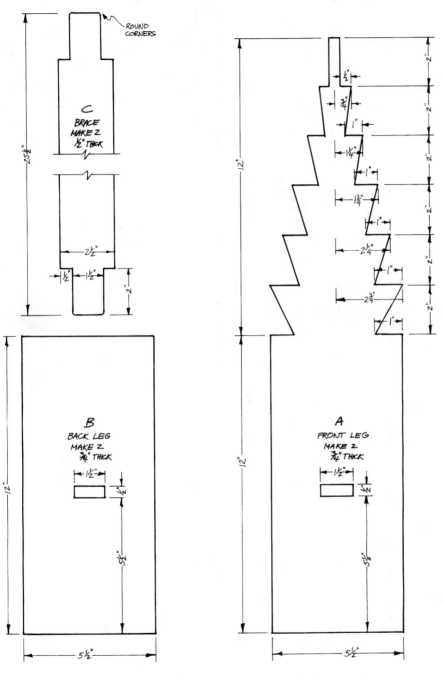

ROUND
CORNERS

C
BRACE
MAKE 2
½" THICK

25½"

2½"

½" · 1½"

2"

2"

¾"

1"

1¼"

1"

1¾"

1"

2¼"

1"

2¾"

1"

12"

2"

2"

2"

2"

2"

2"

B
BACK LEG
MAKE 2
¾" THICK

1½"

½"

5½"

12"

5½"

A
FRONT LEG
MAKE 2
¾" THICK

1½"

¾"

5½"

12"

5½"

Trunk stands 25

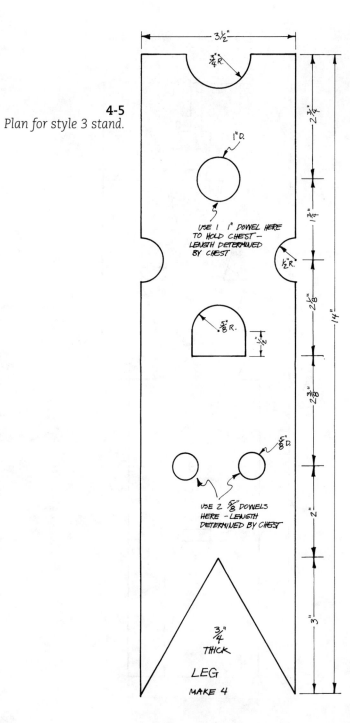

4-5
Plan for style 3 stand.

26 Small household accessories

4-6
*An old chest rests on a
style 1 stand.*

Miniature cart (carreta)

THIS PROJECT is a miniature of the huge ox carts that were used throughout the early Southwest to transport heavy burdens. See Figs. 5-1 and 5-2. Each cart, pulled by a team of oxen, lumbered along on heavy wooden wheels. Seldom were the wheels completely symmetrical. Made of a few large, strong pieces of lumber, a cart was fairly easy to construct and was quite durable. Loads could be tied to the high upright stake sides, and the bed could be easily tipped during loading and unloading. Restored remnants and reproductions of large *carretas* are found in many museums.

The original antique from which I derived these plans is a very small cart now in a Santa Fe museum. It was either a toy or a decoration used in a religious festival of some kind. Small carts with skeleton drivers are a traditional part of the Hispanic religious heritage of the Southwest.

I find the small reproduction an attractive addition to my collection of small antique furniture, dolls, and animals.

For this project, use a wood that is easy to carve, such as pine or basswood.

Materials list

Part	Number Required	Size (inches)
Wheel part (A)	2	$\frac{1}{2} \times 3\frac{1}{8} \times 3\frac{1}{8}$
Wheel part (B)	4	$\frac{3}{16} \times \frac{3}{4} \times \frac{3}{4}$
C and other side pieces (about 60 inches)	4	$\frac{3}{16}$
D	2	$\frac{1}{2} \times \frac{3}{4} \times 6$
E	1	$\frac{1}{2} \times \frac{1}{2} \times 10\frac{7}{8}$
F	2	$\frac{3}{8} \times \frac{1}{2} \times 6$
G	2	$\frac{3}{8} \times \frac{1}{2} \times 4\frac{1}{8}$

Note: Measurements given are finished dimensions.

Miscellaneous:
- Doweling or twigs
- Glue
- Sandpaper
- Gray stain, if desired.

5-1
Miniature cart.

5-2
*Reproduction of a
toy cart.*

5-3
*A large antique cart outside
the Martinez Hacienda
museum in Taos.*

30 Small household accessories

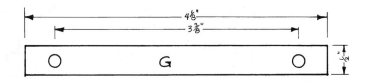

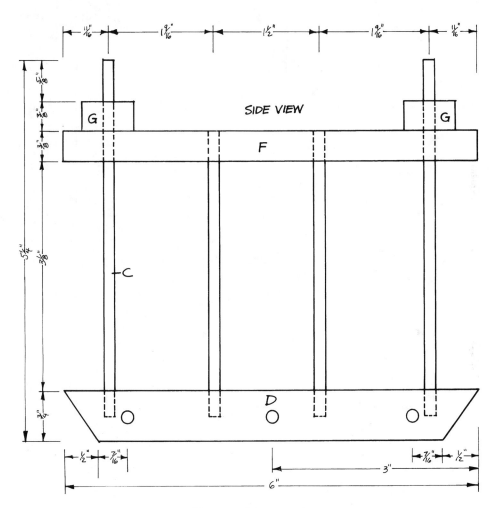

5-4 *Side assembly of a toy cart.*

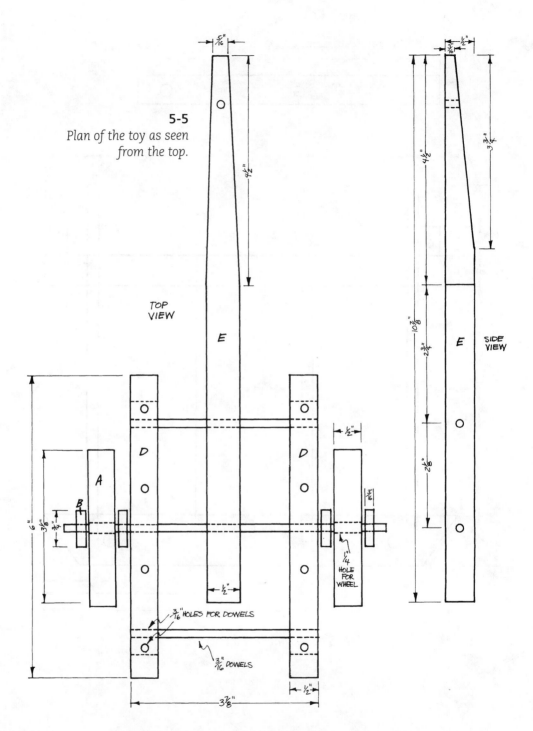

5-5
Plan of the toy as seen
from the top.

$\frac{5}{16}$"

TOP
VIEW

$4\frac{1}{2}$"

E

$\frac{1}{2}$"
$\frac{3}{16}$"

$4\frac{1}{2}$"

$3\frac{3}{4}$"

E

SIDE
VIEW

$10\frac{7}{8}$"

$2\frac{3}{4}$"

$2\frac{1}{8}$"

$\frac{3}{16}$"

A

B

$\frac{3}{8}$"

$3\frac{3}{4}$"

6"

D

D

$\frac{1}{2}$"

$\frac{3}{16}$"

$\frac{1}{4}$"
HOLE
FOR
WHEEL

$\frac{1}{2}$"

$\frac{3}{16}$" HOLES FOR DOWELS

$\frac{3}{16}$" DOWELS

$\frac{1}{2}$"

$3\frac{7}{8}$"

32 Small household accessories

These carts vary in size and in the number of uprights on the sides. Some have strips of wood joined to make a floor. Decide how you want to use the cart, and adjust the plan accordingly. If you want a very rustic look (see the large *caretta* in Fig. 5-3), use twigs instead of dowels and stain a light gray. Much of the construction can be approached as a whittling project.

1. Cut out all major parts. See Figs. 5-4 through 5-6.
2. Drill holes as indicated. Note that the hole drilled through A is larger than the holes drilled in parts B. This allows the wheel to turn freely, while part B stays firmly in place on the axle.
3. Assemble base with parts D and part E. Join by using dowels as crosspieces.
4. Fasten side vertical dowels in side base D.
5. Fasten F top rails onto the uprights.
6. Slide G over upright parts C to hold shape of cart.
7. Finish with gray stain or clear varnish, if desired.

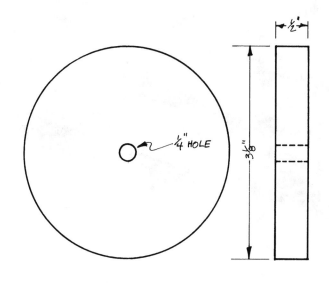

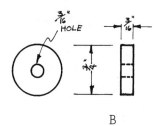

B

5-6
Plan for the wheels.

A

Miniature cart (carreta) 33

Cheese-making tray

WHEN I FIRST saw this piece in a Santa Fe museum, I could not imagine how it had been used. It was carefully carved and too large to carry in one hand by using what I perceived to be the handle. Later I discovered that it was a special tray for making cheese. What we call farmer's cheese was made by letting the curd settle and the whey run out the channel cut into the projection (not a handle) and then into another container. When the whey had drained, the fairly dry curds were probably pressed and shaped into blocks of cheese.

This project, shown in Figs. 6-1 and 6-2, is an interesting one to make. I used a piece of basswood, a fine-grained wood that is easy to carve and chisel.

6-1
Cheese-making tray.

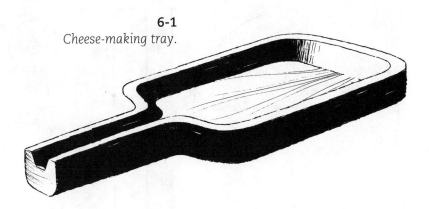

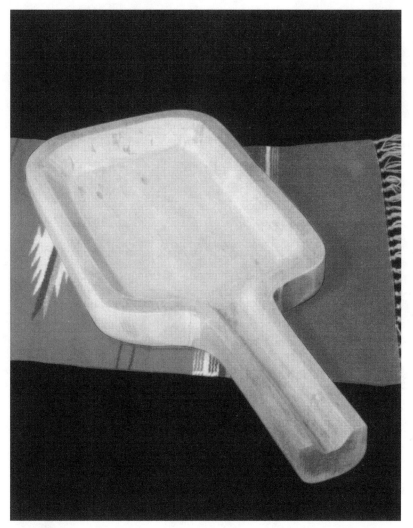

A local mill cut a blank block of basswood for me. You could use another type of wood, but make sure it is even-grained. Unlike the early craftsman who made the original with hand tools, I cut out the outline with my band saw. I carved out the rest with chisel and knife and finished up with sandpaper and elbow grease. I coated the inside with a polyurethane varnish for easy cleaning and left the outside in its natural state.

Today, most people do not make cheese, but the tray is perfect for serving fruit or snacks. I find it a real conversation starter every time I use it.

Materials list
- One 1¾ × 9½ × 22-inch block of wood. Use basswood, or another type that is easy to carve.
- Chisels and mallet
- Sandpaper and palm sander (if you have one)
- Tracing paper
- Nontoxic coating for inside, if desired

Construction tips
1. Trace outline on block of wood, as in Fig. 6-3.
2. Cut out on band saw.
3. Trace side view and gradually chisel and sand to shape, as in Fig. 6-4.
4. Turn block over and trace inner pattern on wood.
5. Cut outlines on wood, gradually chiseling inside slopes around the board and stem. Be careful not to cut below the bottom of the scooped-out area.
6. Gradually chip out center until it reaches the point where you can start leveling the bottom, as in Figs. 6-5 and 6-6. Level with wide chisel.
7. The inside of the cheese tray should be as smooth as possible to resist splintering. A palm sander helps you to finish the bottom faster.
8. The inside can be finished with any nontoxic coating for protection against stains.

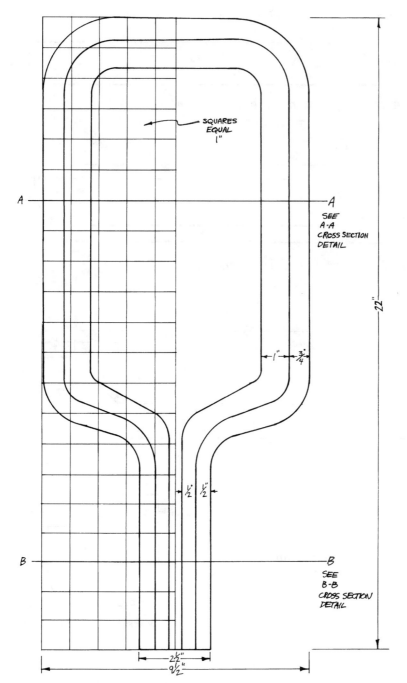

SQUARES
EQUAL
1"

A ——— A
SEE
A-A
CROSS SECTION
DETAIL

1" | 3/4"

22"

1/2" | 1/2"

B ——— B
SEE
B-B
CROSS SECTION
DETAIL

2 1/2"
9 1/2"

6-3
Plan for a tray. Enlarge squares to 1 inch (For cross-section detail, see Fig. 6-6.)

Cheese-making tray 37

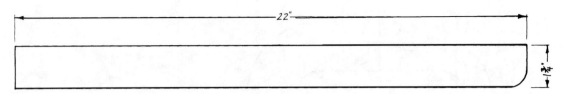

6-4 *Pattern for cutting the base block (side view).*

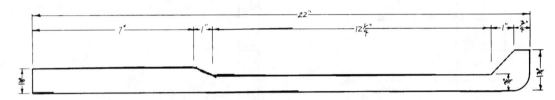

6-5 *Cross section lengthwise through the cheese tray.*

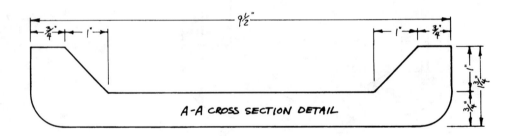

A-A CROSS SECTION DETAIL

6-6
Cross section of the tray through the width.
Note the slope of the interior depression.

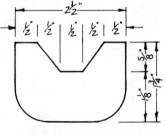

B-B CROSS SECTION DETAIL

38 Small household accessories

Indian hanging cradle (cuna de Indio)

THE ORIGINAL of this unique Indian hanging cradle piqued my interest the moment I saw it. I especially like the stepped design of the headboard and the proportions of the entire piece. See Fig. 7-1. The original is in the Kit Carson House in Taos, New Mexico. The house is furnished with indigenous furniture and other pieces similar to those that Kit Carson may have brought west from his former home.

This pattern for a cradle must have been practical for an Indian mother. She could hang it from an interior ceiling beam or a branch outside. This enabled her to keep the infant nearby as she worked and to rock the cradle gently with an occasional touch of the hand. Raised above the ground, the cradle also protected the baby from snakes and other dangers.

The photo (Fig. 7-2) shows my reproduction cradle, which is stained a soft red. I use it on the porch to hold cascading plants. I hope you will enjoy making and using this project in your own home.

For the wood, use poplar, pine, or cherry.

Materials list

Part	Number Required	Size (inches)
A	1	$\frac{1}{2} \times 7\frac{1}{2} \times 11$
B	2	$\frac{1}{2} \times 5 \times 24$
C	1	$\frac{1}{2} \times 11 \times 29$

Note: Measurements given are finished dimensions.

Miscellaneous
- $\frac{3}{16}$-inch doweling for pinning sections together
- $\frac{1}{4}$-inch rope, about 30 feet, for hanging up cradle
- Thin leather thongs, 4 pieces about 10 inches long
- Sandpaper and glue
- Barn-red paint or stain

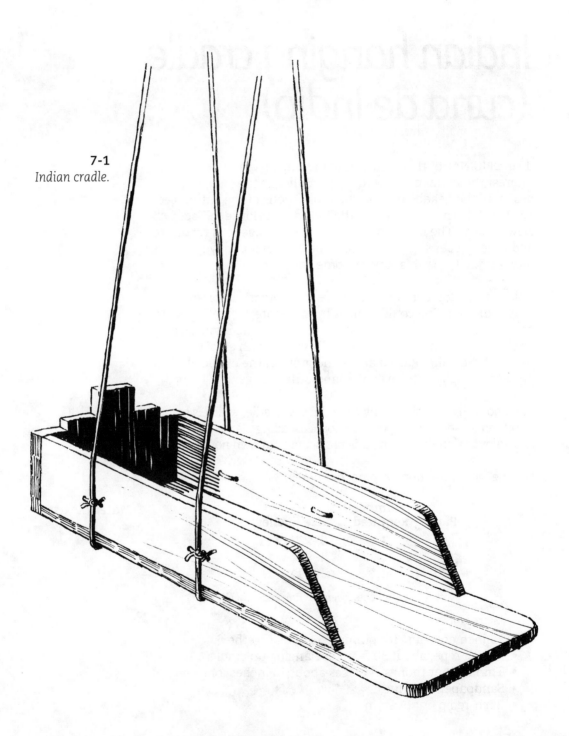

7-1
Indian cradle.

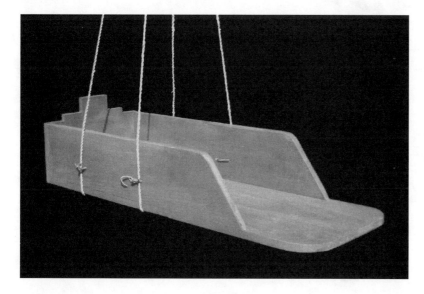

7-2
A reproduction cradle.

1. Cut out all pieces as shown in Fig. 7-3.
2. Glue A and B together.
3. Drill A and B for pinning, and pin.
4. Glue C to A and B assembly.
5. Pin C to top assembly with doweling, as in Fig. 7-4, or use screws countersunk and covered with plugs.
6. Sand and round edges.
7. Paint or stain dull red.
8. Varnish with matte finish, if desired.
9. Tie ropes to cradle with thongs, as in Fig. 7-5.
10. Hang cradle.

Construction tips

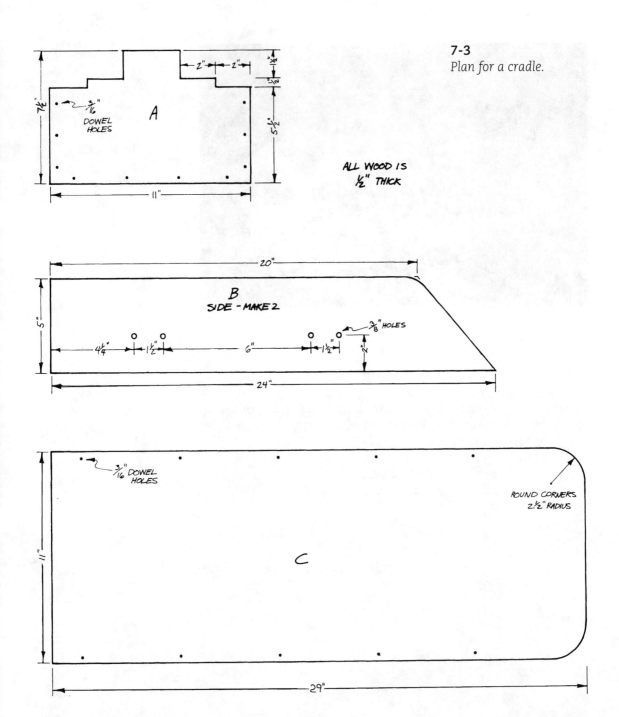

A

3/16"
DOWEL
HOLES

7½"

2" 2"

3/8"

½"

5½"

11"

ALL WOOD IS
½" THICK

20"

B
SIDE - MAKE 2

5"

4¼" 1½" 6" 1½" 3/8" HOLES

2"

24"

3/16" DOWEL
HOLES

ROUND CORNERS
2½" RADIUS

C

11"

29"

42 Small household accessories

7-4
Dowels fasten parts of the cradle together.

7-5
Note how hanging ropes are tied to the cradle with leather thongs.

Indian ladder (escalera de mano)

INDIAN LADDERS of the type in this project are seen throughout the Southwest. See Figs. 8-1 and 8-2. They are still used in Indian pueblos, both for climbing to upper terraces and for hanging out various items to display or dry. I was constantly surprised to see ladders used in so many innovative ways, such as displaying items for sale outside a store.

Originally, the ladder was an essential item for every cliff dwelling and adobe pueblo. The entrance to the home was gained by means of holes far above the ground or on the terrace roof. The residents pulled the ladders up after climbing them, thus making the home less vulnerable to hostile attack.

Ladders were of all sizes and used for many purposes (see Fig. 8-3). I saw some more than 20 feet long and others only 5 or 6 feet in length. A small ladder would be a perfect accessory inside to display quilts and coverlets or outside to dry herbs or chilies.

The Indians used young, straight pines—perhaps lodgepole pines—to make the ladder sides, but any small, straight sapling of any type tree will do. (You could also use stock fencing posts.) The cross rungs are hand carved from strong wood inserted in holes in the rails or lashed onto notches cut in the rails.

8-1 *Indian ladder.*

Materials list

- Side rails 3 inches in diameter and 6 feet or longer, as desired
- Rungs of 2 × 2-inch hardwood, 24 inches wide, or 1½-inch-diameter doweling or handle stock, 24 inches wide—one for at least each 12-inch length of side rail

8-3
A ladder in use at cliff ruins.

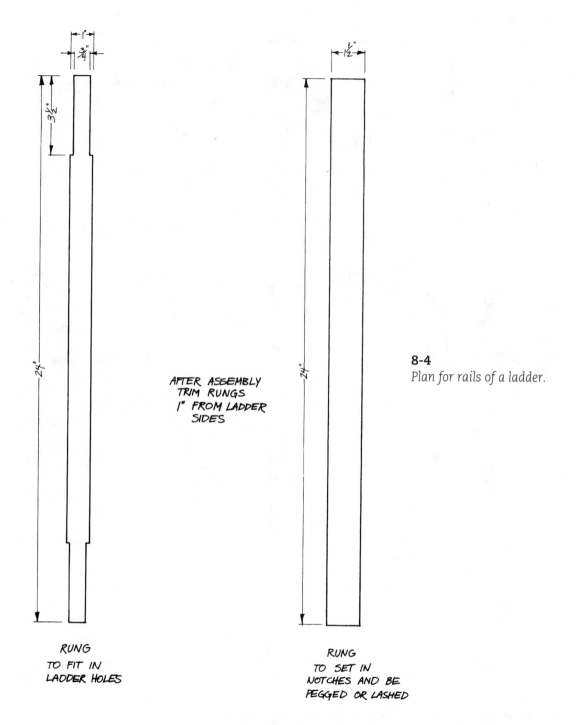

1"

¾"

3½"

24"

AFTER ASSEMBLY
TRIM RUNGS
1" FROM LADDER
SIDES

½"

24"

8-4
Plan for rails of a ladder.

RUNG
TO FIT IN
LADDER HOLES

RUNG
TO SET IN
NOTCHES AND BE
PEGGED OR LASHED

Indian ladder (escalera de mano) 47

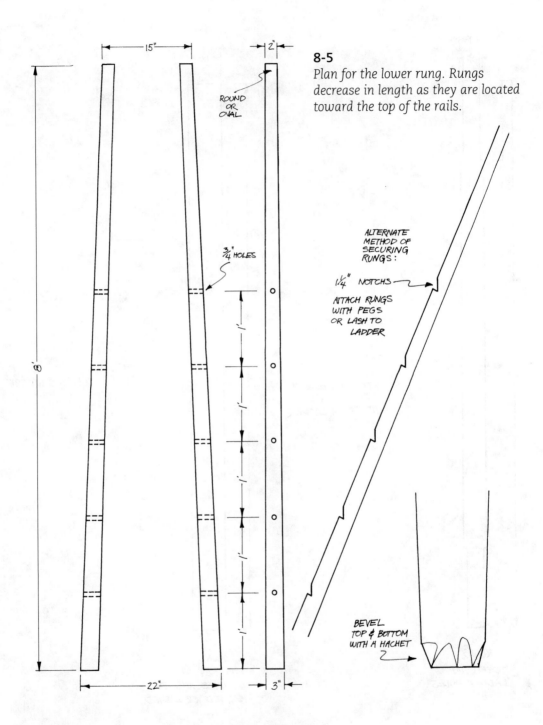

15"

2"

ROUND
OR
OVAL

8-5
Plan for the lower rung. Rungs decrease in length as they are located toward the top of the rails.

¾" HOLES

ALTERNATE
METHOD OF
SECURING
RUNGS:

1¼" NOTCHS

ATTACH RUNGS
WITH PEGS
OR LASH TO
LADDER

8'

1'

1'

1'

1'

1'

22"

3"

BEVEL
TOP & BOTTOM
WITH A HACHET

48 Small household accessories

1. Shape the rails and smooth them slightly.
2. Lay out the rails on the floor in the configuration you desire. See Fig. 8-4.
3. Mark locations of holes for the rungs. Be sure to mark them in straight lines.
4. Drill holes through the rails.
5. Lay the rungs across the rails in position and mark the actual lengths needed. See the plan for the lower rung in Fig. 8-5. Rungs will decrease in length as they near the top of the ladder, but the ends will extend past the side rails (Fig. 8-6).
6. Shape the rungs.
7. Insert rungs into rails.
8. Wedge to tighten, if necessary.
9. Use as desired (see Fig. 8-7).

8-6
Note how rungs extend through the rails

1. Follow construction tips 1, 2, and 3.
2. Cut notches in side rails.
3. Prepare rungs as in construction tips 5 and 6.
4. Lay rungs across side rails and lash or nail in place.

8-7
*A ladder in use at a modern
hotel in Santa Fe.*

Three-legged stool (escabel)

THE LITTLE STOOL shown in Figs. 9-1 and 9-2 is a true pioneer seat. Rough-cut yet practical, it can be made and used on the spot. Its design totally lacks sophistication, but it has a functional, rugged charm. The stool I copied for this project has a well-worn top and handle that attests to years of usefulness.

The pattern (Fig. 9-3) is more a method of construction than an actual measured pattern. Indeed, you may have a section of log with an entirely different dimension, so do not try to follow my measurements closely for the main piece that makes the seat. It can be larger or smaller without compromising the authenticity of the finished project. It is important to use a

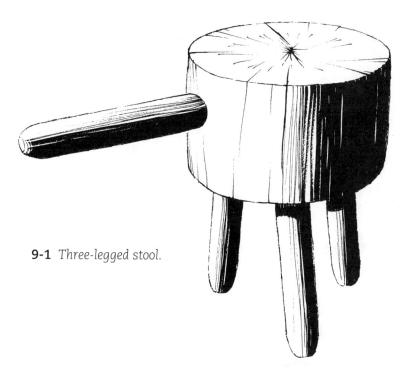

9-1 *Three-legged stool.*

good solid section of tree trunk and to have legs and a handle strong enough to support it.

These stools are wonderful for the garden or patio. Use them to provide extra seating or as little tables.

Use pine or poplar for this project.

Materials list
- 1 piece of log, 10 to 12 inches in diameter and 4 to 6 inches thick
- 4 pieces, 1½ inches in diameter and 10 inches long

Construction tips
1. Trim bark off log for section A.
2. Shave or sand log to smooth it.
3. Cut handle for section B.
4. Drill hole in one side of A for section B. See Fig. 9-3.
5. Drill three holes for legs in bottom of A. Note: These holes are drilled at an angle. Check the pattern.

6. Cut leg sections C and shape. See Fig. 9-4.
7. Sand or chisel top of A to make the seat indentation, as in Fig. 9-5.
8. Insert legs and handle into A.
9. Glue or wedge to tighten, if necessary.

9-3
Plan for making a stool.

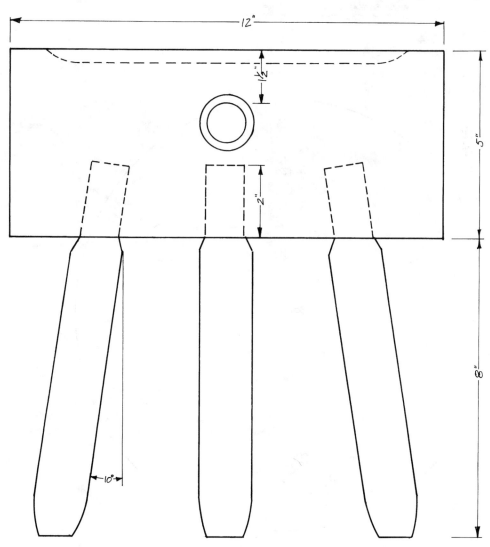

Three-legged stool (escabel) 53

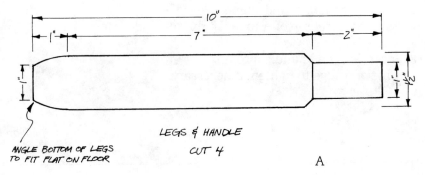

ANGLE BOTTOM OF LEGS
TO FIT FLAT ON FLOOR

LEGS & HANDLE
CUT 4

A

9-4
*Plan for the legs and handle
(A) and plan showing their
placement on the stool (B).*

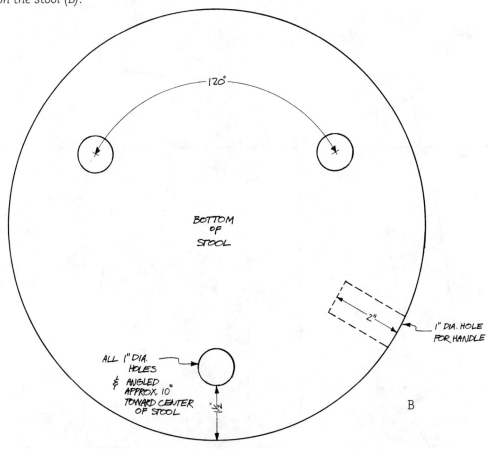

120°

BOTTOM
OF
STOOL

ALL 1" DIA.
HOLES
& ANGLED
APPROX. 10°
TOWARD CENTER
OF STOOL

1" DIA. HOLE
FOR HANDLE

2"

B

54 Small household accessories

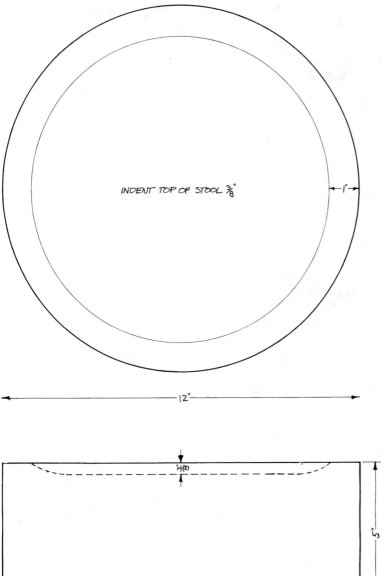

INDENT TOP OF STOOL 3/8"

←1"→

9-5
*Plan for indenting the top of
the stool with a chisel or
sanding disk.*

←————————————12"————————————→

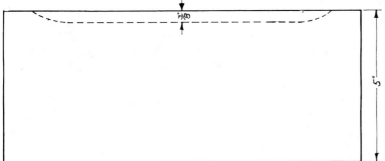

3/8"

5"

Three-legged stool (escabel) 55

Wooden hanging rods

A DISTINCTIVE decorating feature in homes of the Southwest consisted of rugs and blankets hung on walls and over windows and doors. This practice kept heat in or out and provided privacy. Many interior rooms had doorways but no doors, and the hanging blankets allowed an easy, colorful separation between rooms. Rugs and carpets were also hung on the plain adobe walls as decorative elements, much as we hang a painting today.

The early housewives expressed much creativity in their own weaving and in their selection of beautiful Indian weavings. The Southwesterners made and appreciated woven goods as practical household pieces that were enhanced by fine craftsmanship and artistry of design. This meld of art, craftsmanship, and practicality was similar to the Easterners' practice of quiltmaking and their appreciation of decorative quilt patterns and fine stitching.

Wooden hanging rods held the rugs and woven blankets. See Figs. 10-1 and 10-2. The rods were made in different lengths, according to the width of the work to be hung.

A rod could be used to display any woven piece, a small quilt, or perhaps a rya rug. The rug is fastened to the groove in the back, and the rod is attached to the wall with screws or pegs. Measure the top of the piece you wish to hang. Add eight inches and make your wooden rod to that measure. Repeat the incised decoration to fill the space between the ends of the rod. Your hanging will be displayed to show its beauty to full advantage.

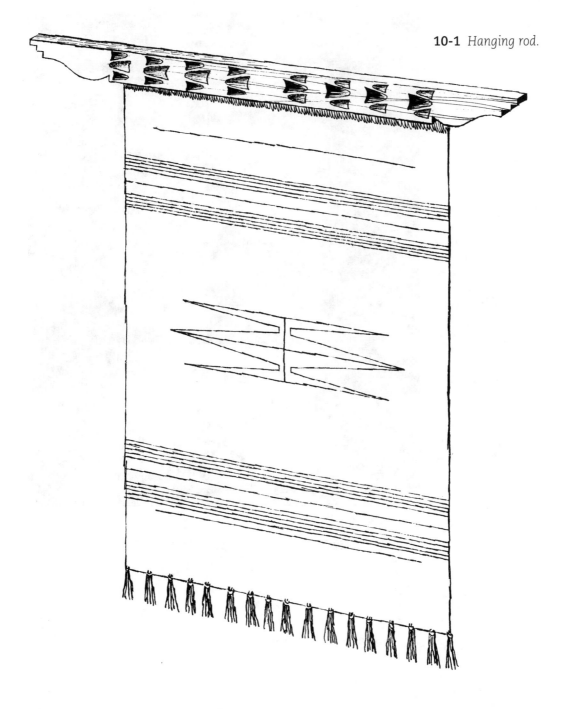

Wooden hanging rods 57

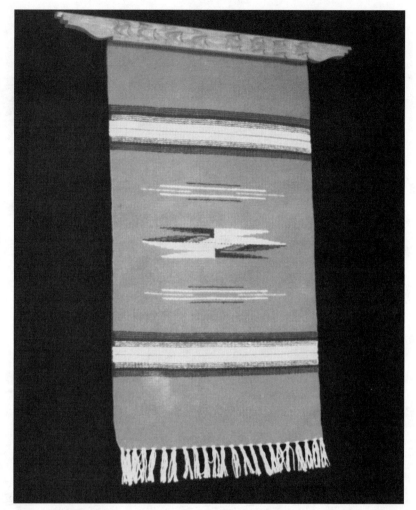

10-2
A reproduction rod.

Be sure to use pine or another type of even-grained wood that is easy to carve.

Materials list
- 1 piece, ¾ × 2 inches × desired length (determine length by measuring width of rug or blanket to be hung and adding 8 inches)
- ½ × ¾-inch round chisels
- Mallet
- Wood stain

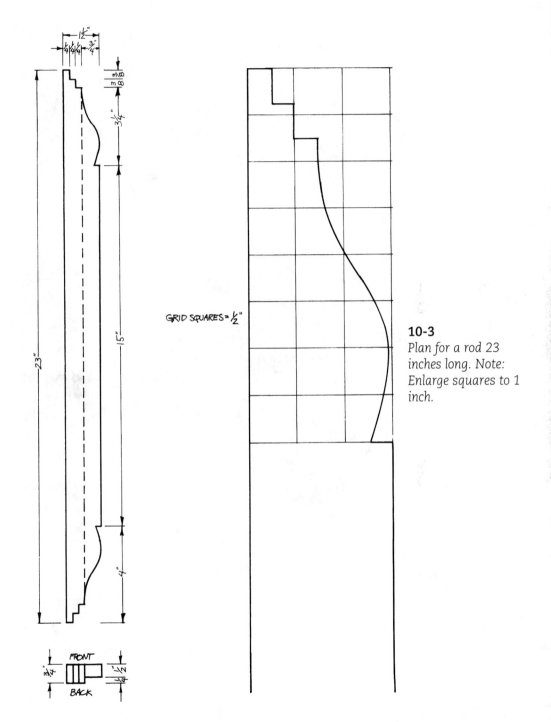

GRID SQUARES = $\frac{1}{2}$"

10-3
Plan for a rod 23 inches long. Note: Enlarge squares to 1 inch.

FRONT

BACK

Wooden hanging rods 59

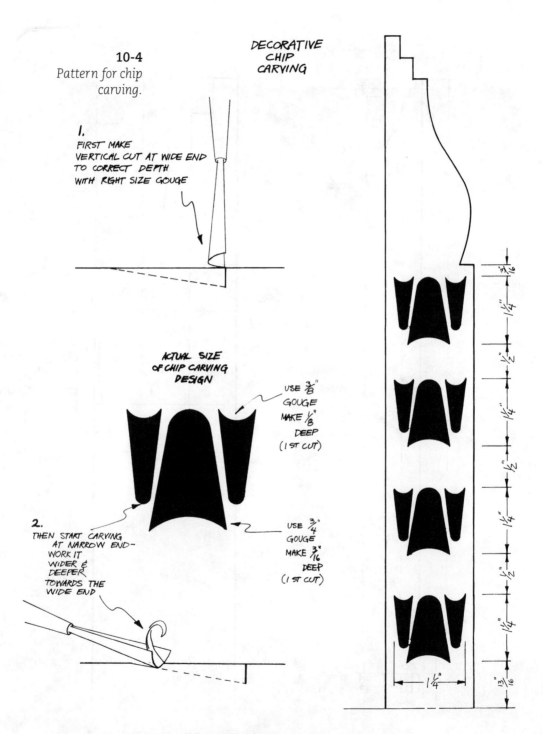

10-4
Pattern for chip carving.

DECORATIVE CHIP CARVING

1.
FIRST MAKE VERTICAL CUT AT WIDE END TO CORRECT DEPTH WITH RIGHT SIZE GOUGE

ACTUAL SIZE OF CHIP CARVING DESIGN

USE $\frac{3}{8}$" GOUGE MAKE $\frac{1}{8}$" DEEP (1ST CUT)

2.
THEN START CARVING AT NARROW END — WORK IT WIDER & DEEPER TOWARDS THE WIDE END

USE $\frac{3}{4}$" GOUGE MAKE $\frac{3}{16}$" DEEP (1ST CUT)

$\frac{3}{16}$"
$1\frac{1}{4}$"
$\frac{1}{2}$"
$\frac{1}{4}$"
$\frac{1}{2}$"
$1\frac{1}{4}$"
$\frac{1}{2}$"
$1\frac{1}{4}$"
$\frac{3}{16}$"

$1\frac{1}{4}$"

60 Small household accessories

1. Starting at each end, lay out pattern on wood and cut out. See Fig. 10-3.
2. Rout groove in back as shown on plan.
3. Trace chip carving pattern on front, as in Fig. 10-4. Start at ends and work toward the center.
4. Chip carve design with chisels and mallet. See Figs. 10-5 through 10-7.
5. Sand.
6. Paint stain on and rub it off to bring out the pattern. See Fig. 10-8.
7. Drill holes in ends for hanging. Figure 10-9 shows detail of the back prior to drilling the holes.

Construction tips

10-5
First, make a vertical chip.

10-6
Next, start a shallow cut at the far end of chip from the first cut.

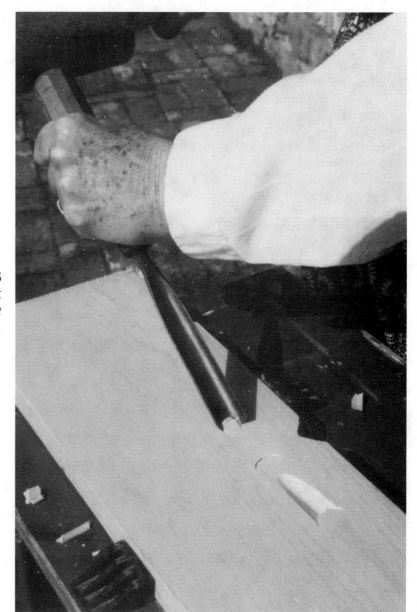

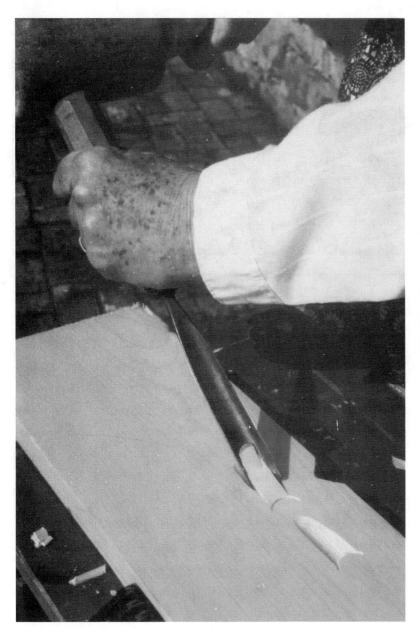

10-7
Finish the cut by pressing deeper as you near the first vertical cut. Remove the chip in one piece, if possible.

10-8
Detail of chip carvings before holes are drilled in the ends for hanging.

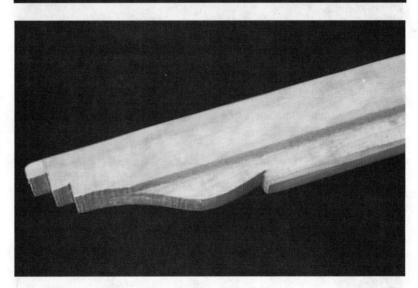

10-9
Detail of back of the rod showing groove where the rug is attached. (Note that holes for hanging the rod have not been drilled.)

Furniture

The patterns in this book are derived from antiques of the Southwest that date from the seventeenth through nineteenth centuries. Similar patterns and designs have been used in rural areas of the region throughout its history. They are now in a renaissance of popularity, not only in the Southwest but wherever handcrafted pieces of authentic design are appreciated.

According to today's standards, the homes of early Southwestern settlers were sparsely furnished. A house may have had one room or several. The typical adobe room had a low door and a tiny, high window to admit light. The ceiling was made of rushes or twigs laid over rough-hewn beams. Doorways were sometimes covered with rugs or blankets hung over rods in order to give a little privacy and to preserve warmth.

Often, a family had a small chest that was raised off the floor in Spanish fashion by means of a wooden stand. Frequently, referred to as a bride's chest, it was decorated with a carved or painted design and certainly became the focus of a room.

The room might also contain a small table holding a Bible and writing supplies, a chair, a bench, a sconce for candles, a shelf or two, and perhaps a corner fireplace to provide heat. The small tables were never used for dining. Meals were taken picnic style. Chairs were few and were reserved for visiting dignitaries, priests, or the head of the household. Other family members sat on small stools or benches.

Shelf assemblies of all sizes and shapes were important features of colonial rooms. They were suspended from the rafters by ropes or fastened to pegs driven into the wall.

Just as in the early settlers' homes in other regions of the country, most of the furniture and accessories were made by a member of the household or a visiting artisan. Because wood was soft and scarce and tools simple, each piece was crafted slowly and carefully to fulfill a specific need. In the rural areas of the Southwest, the designs, plans, and methods of making furniture were passed down from generation to generation.

This continuance of old ways among craftsmen makes it very difficult to date precisely when a piece was made, but we can deduce much from the marks left by the craftsman's chisel and knife. The tightness of the mortises, the beauty of the carving, and even the errors made in cutting tell a story to the trained eye. Every handmade item reveals much about the character traits of the maker—patience, ability, and caring. The execution of the carving and painting also reveal the maker's artistry and background.

The craftspeople of the Southwest were interested in the elegant, colorful effect of their work as much as in its usefulness. Details of design were often executed in a loose, individualistic style, rather than in a stamped-out, precise manner. For instance, decorative splats in the back of a chair differ from each other, or scallops cut out along a shelf are not precisely identical, but these features produce a harmony of design that is attractive and distinctive. The casual approach to nonfunctional parts and meticulous attention to joining are characteristic of the style of the Southwest.

The charming, unique style of these country pieces blends well with any other functional country style, whether antique or contemporary.

Bench (tarima)

BENCHES similar to this project were used in other colonial areas of this country as much as they were in the Southwest. See Figs. 11-1 and 11-2. In fact, simple wooden benches are still common fixtures in all rural areas of the world. Easy to construct, movable, and adaptable to many uses, benches have been the most popular form of seating for hundreds of years. They are used inside and out for meetings, dining, and working. You will certainly find many uses for this piece.

If you have made reproductions of farm benches from other areas, you will notice a strong family resemblance. The early Hispanic colonial benches were often built along heavier lines. For a more rustic appearance that is appropriate for porch or outside use, you can use a thicker wood throughout. A bench constructed of redwood would be perfect for the garden or beside a pool.

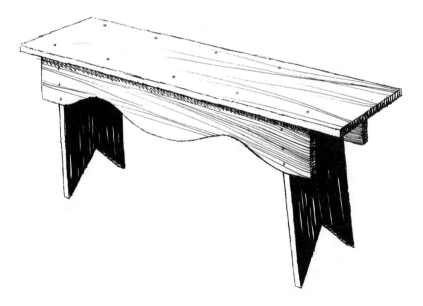

11-1
Bench.

11-2
A reproduction bench.

Materials list

Part	Number Required	Size (inches)
Leg (A)	2	¾ × 9¼ × 17
Braces (B)	2	¾ × 3½ × 7¾
Seat (C)	1	¾ × 11 × 41
Aprons (D)	2	¾ × 5 × 35

Note: Measurements given are finished dimensions.

Miscellaneous:
- ⁷⁄₁₆-inch doweling for pinning, or 1¼-inch wood screws and plugs to cover
- Glue

Construction tips

1. Cut out pieces A through D and sand. See Figs. 11-3 through 11-6.
2. Angle legs at top and bottom. Angle ledge on which aprons will sit.
3. Attach braces to legs with glue and screws or pins, as in Fig. 11-7.
4. Attach aprons to legs with glue and pins. See Fig. 11-8.
5. Attach seat to bottom assembly with pins or screws set at opposing angles.
6. Sand edges until well rounded.
7. Finish, as desired, with wood sealer, stain, or paint. Be sure to sand between coats.

11-3 Total bench assembly from the front.

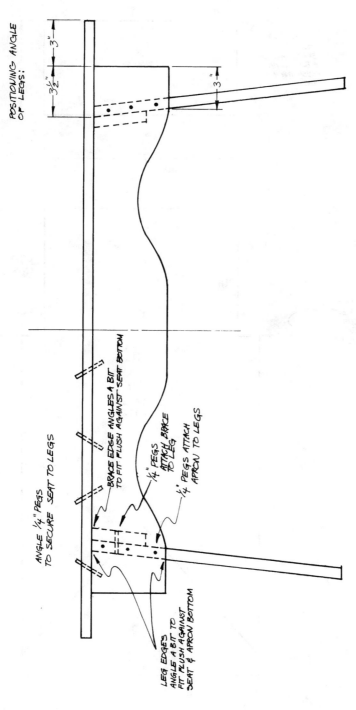

POSITIONING ANGLE
OF LEGS:

3"

3½"

3"

ANGLE ¼" PEGS
TO SECURE SEAT TO LEGS

BRACE EDGE ANGLES A BIT
TO FIT FLUSH AGAINST SEAT BOTTOM

¼" PEGS
ATTACH BRACE
TO LEG

¼" PEGS ATTACH
APRON TO LEGS

LEG EDGES
ANGLE A BIT TO
FIT FLUSH AGAINST
SEAT & APRON BOTTOM

Bench (tarima) 69

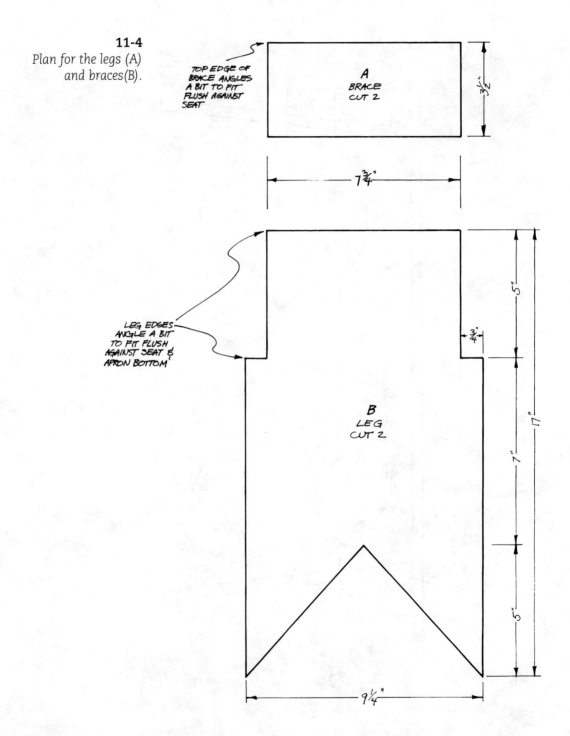

11-4
*Plan for the legs (A)
and braces(B).*

TOP EDGE OF
BRACE ANGLES
A BIT TO FIT
FLUSH AGAINST
SEAT

A
BRACE
CUT 2

3½"

7¾"

LEG EDGES
ANGLE A BIT
TO FIT FLUSH
AGAINST SEAT &
APRON BOTTOM

¾"

5"

B
LEG
CUT 2

17"

7"

5"

9¼"

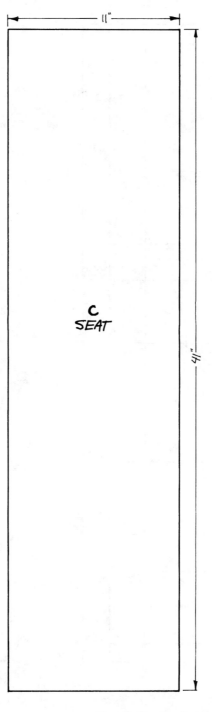

11-5
Plan for the seat.

C
SEAT

11"

41"

Bench (tarima) 71

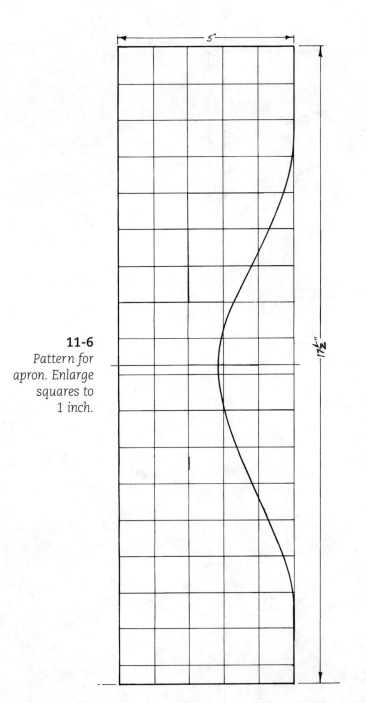

11-6
Pattern for apron. Enlarge squares to 1 inch.

D

PATTERN FOR APRON
(½ PATTERN SHOWN – REPEAT THIS PATTERN)
SQUARES = 1"

5"

17½"

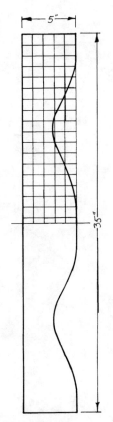

5"

35"

FULL APRON
SHOWING PATTERN FOR RIGHT SIDE

11-7
Detail of brace under the bench. Note optional screws.

11-8
Note pins that hold the apron to the leg.

Hanging shelves with pegs (alazen)

THE ORIGINAL of this shelf assembly hangs against a whitewashed adobe wall in a Taos museum house. See Figs. 12-1 and 12-2. I imagine that it looks much the same as it did more than a century ago. The equivalent of a wall cabinet and a closet, it holds plates, jars, kitchen utensils, and articles of clothing. Although the original has only two shelves and one pegged backboard, you could easily add more in the same manner.

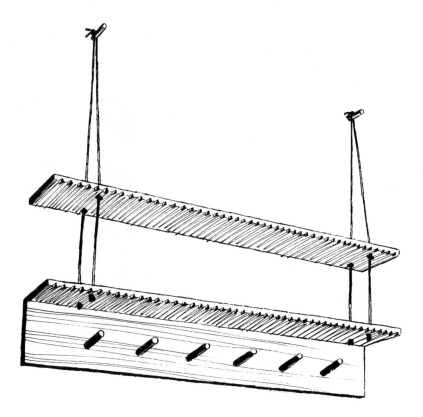

12-1
Shelf assembly.

The old shelves have chipped notches cut along the front edges. The edges were also painted, but the rest of the shelf assembly appears to have been left unpainted.

I can imagine an early housewife, anxious to put her house in order, asking her husband for more shelves. Whether she received shelves of this pattern or another, I am sure she put them to good use.

For this project, use pine.

Materials list

Part	Number Required	Size (inches)
A & B	2	¾ × 9 × 50
C	1	¾ × 7½ × 50

Miscellaneous
- Doweling, ¾ × 33 inches, for pegs
- ¼-inch rope, about 20 feet
- Sandpaper
- Glue
- Red paint and white paint
- ⅜-inch doweling or square pegs for joining B and C together
- Straight-edge chisels, with edge of ¾ inch, and mallet

76 Furniture

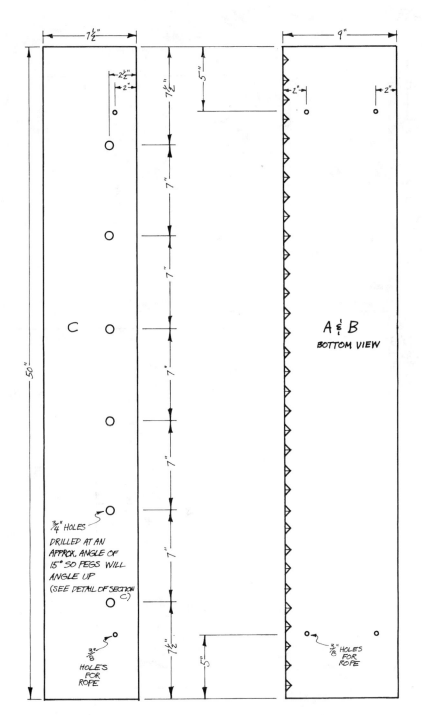

7½"

2½"
2"

7½"

5"

9"

2"   2"

50"

7"

7"

C   ○

7"

A & B
BOTTOM VIEW

7"

¾" HOLES
DRILLED AT AN
APPROX. ANGLE OF
15° SO PEGS WILL
ANGLE UP
(SEE DETAIL OF SECTION
C)

7"

7½"

5"

⅜" HOLES
FOR
ROPE

⅜" HOLES
FOR
ROPE

12-3
Plan for the shelves and
backboard.

Hanging shelves with pegs (alazen) 77

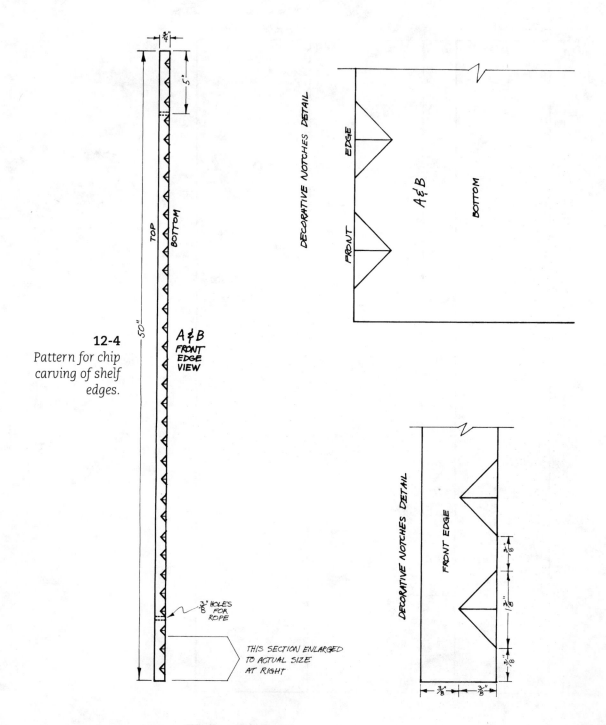

12-4
Pattern for chip carving of shelf edges.

DECORATIVE NOTCHES DETAIL

A & B
FRONT
EDGE
VIEW

TOP

BOTTOM

50"

5"

3/4"

3/8" HOLES
FOR
ROPE

THIS SECTION ENLARGED
TO ACTUAL SIZE
AT RIGHT

DECORATIVE NOTCHES DETAIL

EDGE

FRONT

A & B

BOTTOM

DECORATIVE NOTCHES DETAIL

FRONT EDGE

3/8"

3/8"

3/8"

3/8"

3/8"

78 Furniture

This is a nice project for practicing wood chip decoration. The uneven chip cuts in the original pieces of the Southwest added to their charm. Precision is not as important as the total effect, which should be loose and flowing.

1. Cut base shapes. See Figs. 12-3 and 12-4.
2. Drill holes for pegs and ropes. Holes for pegs are set at an angle (see Fig. 12-3).
3. Chip carve front edges of boards with chisel and mallet. (see Fig. 12-4) Start at right edge of desired cut. Cut and angle toward the middle. Then start at left and cut again toward the middle to complete the chip. At first, it may take several strikes to finish a cut, but as you improve you will be able to complete each side of a chip with one strike. See Figs. 12-5 through 12-7.
4. Sand boards.
5. Round pegs at one end. The opposite end will be cut off flush after pegs are mounted in backboard.
6. Fasten B to C with glue and pins set at opposing angles. Clamp and let set up for a day.
7. Fasten pegs in place on backboard. Glue or wedge, if desired.
8. Paint backs, shelves, and pegs white to get whitewash effect. Rub down or sand after painting.

12-5
Note chip pattern cut in the shelf edges. The shelf has been painted, but the edges are still unpainted.

Hanging shelves with pegs (alazen) 79

12-6
Starting to cut chips
with a chisel.

9. Paint front edges red.
10. Sand all edges a little for a worn look.
11. String and knot with ropes, as shown in Fig. 12-8. Hang up and enjoy.

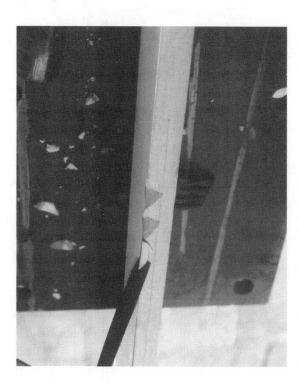

12-7
Completing a chip by cutting from the other side toward the center.

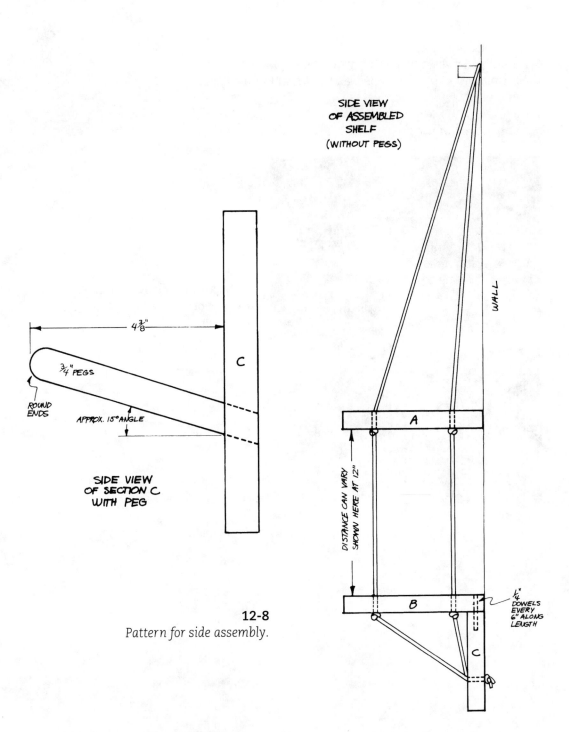

SIDE VIEW
OF **ASSEMBLED**
SHELF
(WITHOUT PEGS)

WALL

$4\frac{3}{8}$"

$\frac{3}{4}$" PEGS

ROUND
ENDS

APPROX. 15° ANGLE

C

SIDE VIEW
OF SECTION C
WITH PEG

A

DISTANCE CAN VARY
SHOWN HERE AT 12"

B

C

$\frac{1}{4}$"
DOWELS
EVERY
6" ALONG
LENGTH

12-8
Pattern for side assembly.

82 Furniture

Shelf with scalloped backboard (alazen)

OF ALL THE wonderful items I saw in the Southwest, this shelf is my favorite (Fig. 13-1). The original (Fig. 13-2) is in the Kit Carson House in Taos. A multipurpose piece, it has pegs for clothes, water bottles, and chilies and a shelf to hold pots and jars. The shelf hangs on pegs driven into the adobe wall. Of particular interest is the decorated back section, which has scallops cut along the top and a painted design on the scalloped edge. The irregularity of the scalloped backboard, with its rustic charm, sets this project apart from most other shelf patterns of the period.

Shelves of all kinds were common in the homes of the early settlers. Easily constructed shelves took the place of closets or wardrobes, which required more wood, were difficult to make,

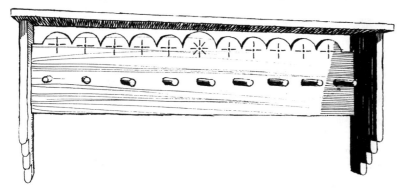

13-1
Shelf assembly with scallops.

13-2
Original shelf hanging in the Kit Carson Museums in Taos, New Mexico.

and were therefore scarce. Most shelf assemblies from this early period were easily taken from one room to another or from one home to another if the family moved.

Use pine for this project.

Materials list

Part	Number Required	Size (inches)
A	1	³/₄ × 7 × 50
B	1	¾ × 9³/₄ × 48
C	2	¾ × 5 × 18½

Note: Measurements given are finished dimensions.

Miscellaneous:
- Doweling, ⅜ inch, enough for joinings
- 6 pegs, 6 inches long, cut from ¾-inch doweling.

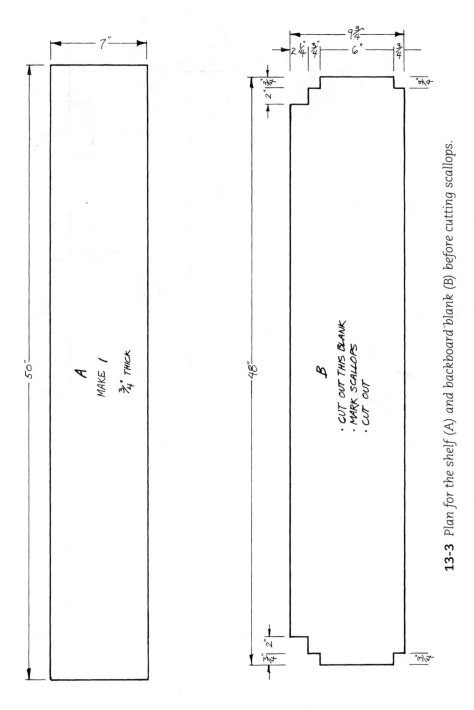

A

MAKE 1

¾" THICK

7"

50"

9¾"

2¼"   ¾"   6"   ¾"

2"¾"

¾"

B

• CUT OUT THIS BLANK
• MARK SCALLOPS
• CUT OUT

48"

¾" 2"

¾"

13-3 *Plan for the shelf (A) and backboard blank (B) before cutting scallops.*

Shelf with scalloped backboard (alazen) 85

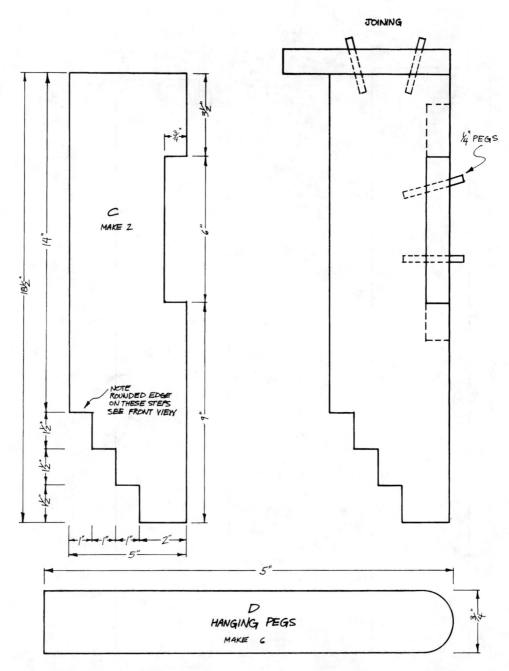

13-4 *Plan for the sides (C) and pegs (D).*

86 Furniture

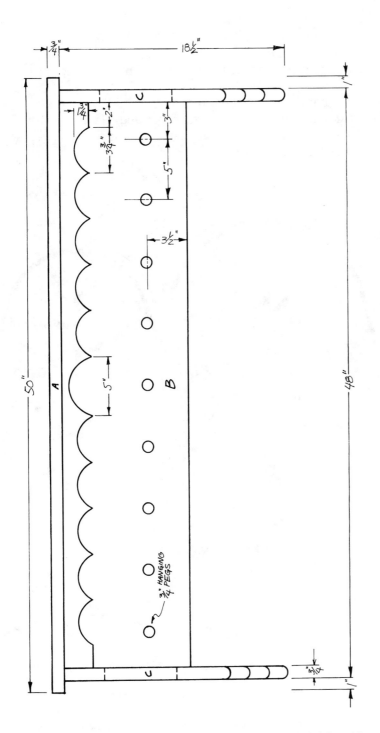

13-5
*Front view showing scallops
on the backboard.*

Shelf with scalloped backboard (alazen) 87

Construction tips

1. Cut all main pieces. See Figs. 13-3, and 13-4.
2. Carve trim on backboard (B), as in Fig. 13-5.
3. Sand all pieces; be sure to shape backboard scallops as shown.
4. Paint backboard design red and blue. See Fig. 13-6.
5. Drill holes for pegs and insert pegs; wedge, if necessary.
6. Assemble shelves; fastening parts together with dowels set at angles. Glue, if desired.

13-6
Patterns for decoration. Also, paint the edges of the scallops on the backboard.

Bench with solid back (banco)

THIS PROJECT is derived from an old bench owned by El Rancho de las Golondrinas. See Fig. 14-1. El Rancho, a *paraje* on the El Camino Royale, was passed down through many generations of the same family. It is now a museum of colonial life. I saw a reproduction of this bench on one of the porches and found it a most comfortable place to sit while resting weary feet.

The original bench, dating back to the first quarter of the nineteenth century, has had its legs replaced. The reproduction, shown in Fig. 14-2, has legs of a type that may have been on the original. Unlike most Southwestern antiques, the joining on the original was with handmade, square-headed nails, rather than mortise and tenon.

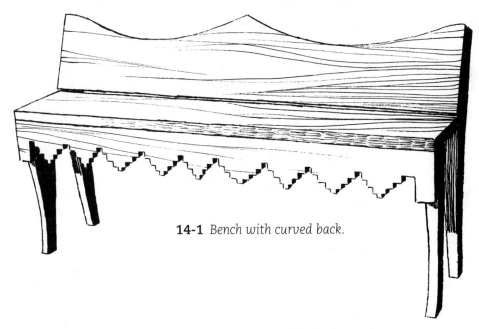

14-1 *Bench with curved back.*

Bench with solid back (banco) 89

I find the curved back and stepped design of the apron
particularly attractive (see Fig. 14-3). Very graceful, even
though unpainted, and rustic in execution, this bench would be
perfect for occasional seating on a porch or in a hall or garden.
It fits into almost any decor.

You can use pine, teak, or mahogany for this project.

Materials list

Part	Number Required	Size (inches)
A (back)	1	¾ × 10 × 61
B (seat)	1	¾ × 13 × 61
C (front apron)	1	¾ × 5 × 61
D (front legs)	2	1½ × 3½ × 17
E (back legs)	2	1½ × 6 × 28
F (back apron)	1	¾ × 5 × 58
G (sides)	2	1½ × 5 × 13

Note: Measurements given are finished dimensions.

Miscellaneous:
Original bench was fastened with handmade nails deadened on
inside to hold. I suggest the use of screws, with plugs to cover

for fastening apron to legs, back to back legs, and seat to side. Bolts can be used to fasten legs to sides G and then covered with plugs.

1. Cut and sand basic pieces. See Figs. 14-3 through 14-8.
2. Draw pattern for front apron on wood and cut out. See Fig. 14-9.
3. Fasten legs to G's with screws or bolts.
4. Fasten F to back of G's and C to front of legs.
5. Add seat and back, and fasten with screws or dowels.
6. Sand well, rounding corners. Wax or varnish, if desired.

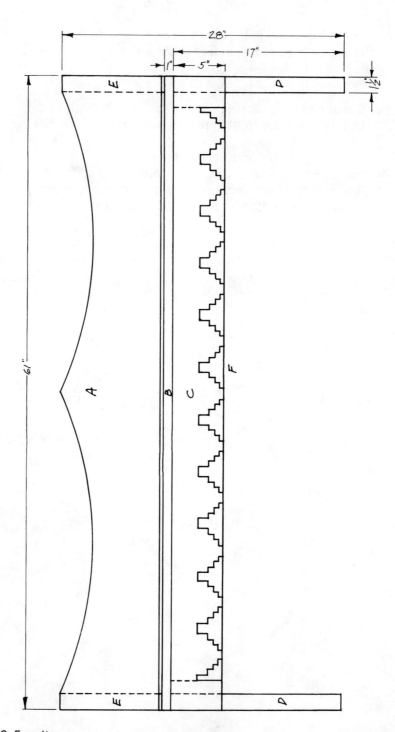

14-3
Front view of the bench assembly. A, back; B, seat; C, front apron; D, front legs; E, back legs; F, back apron.

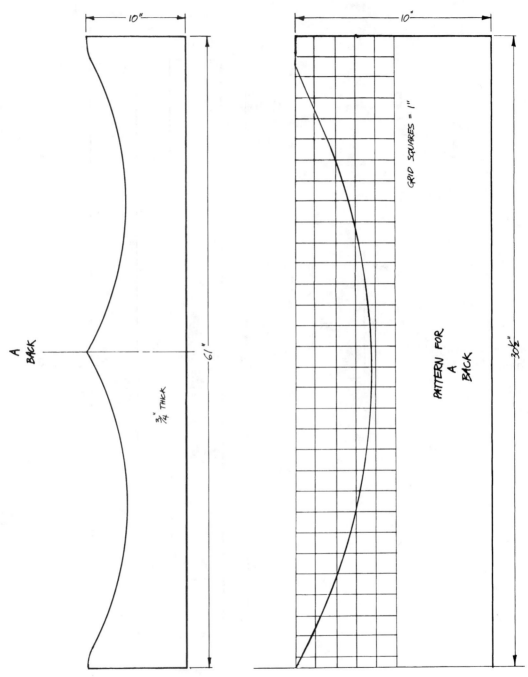

14-4 *Pattern for the back (A). EnLarge squares to 1 inch.*

Bench with solid back (banco) 93

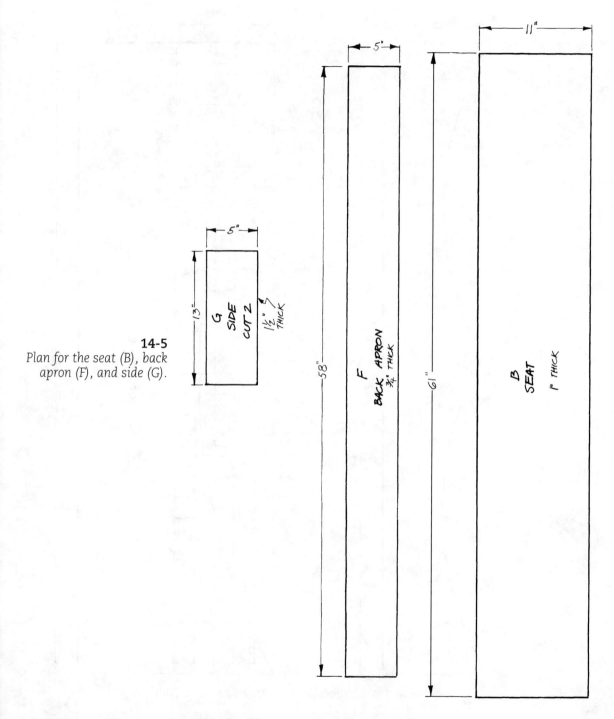

14-5
Plan for the seat (B), back apron (F), and side (G).

G
SIDE
CUT 2

5"

13"

1½"
THICK

F
BACK APRON
¾" THICK

5"

58"

B
SEAT
1" THICK

11"

61"

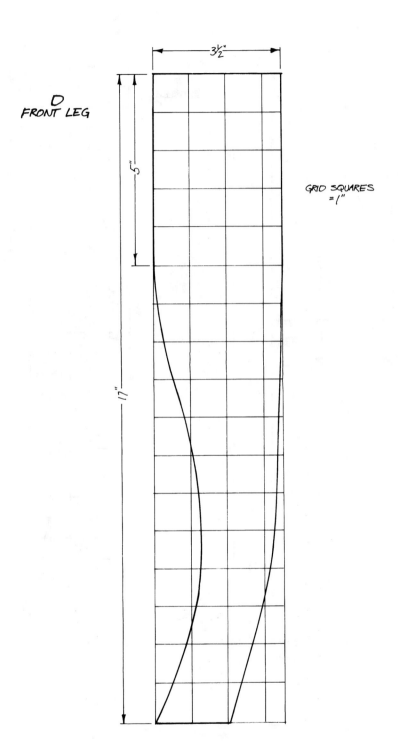

D
FRONT LEG

3½"

5"

17"

GRID SQUARES
= 1"

14-6
Plan for the front legs (D).
Enlarge squares to 1 inch.

Bench with solid back (banco) 95

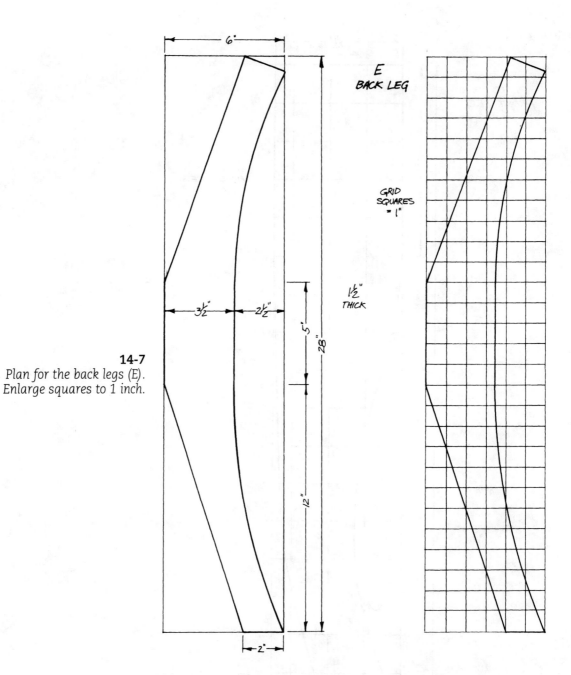

6"

E
BACK LEG

GRID
SQUARES
= 1"

3½"   2½"

1½"
THICK

5'

28"

14-7
Plan for the back legs (E).
Enlarge squares to 1 inch.

12"

2"

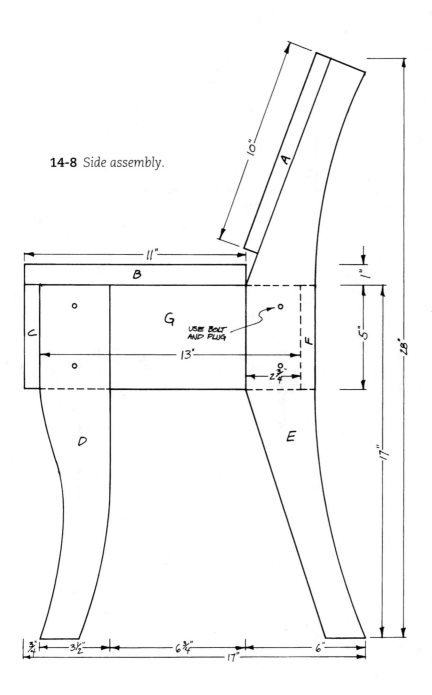

14-8 Side assembly.

10"

A

11"

B

C

G   USE BOLT
     AND PLUG

13'

2 ¾"

D

E

F

1"

5"

28"

17"

¾"   3½"   6¾"   6"

17"

Bench with solid back (banco) 97

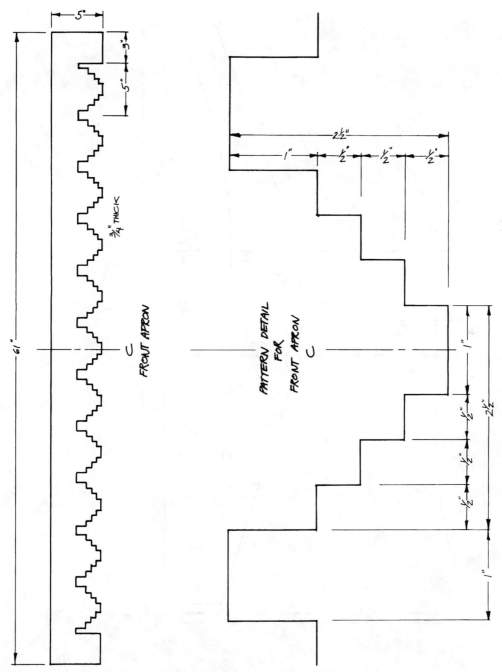

14-9 *Plan for cutting the front apron (C).*

98 Furniture

Love seat with decorative splats

THIS SETTEE (Fig. 15-1) is an example of the fully developed colonial style of the Southwest. (The armless chair described in Chapter 16 also demonstrates this style.)

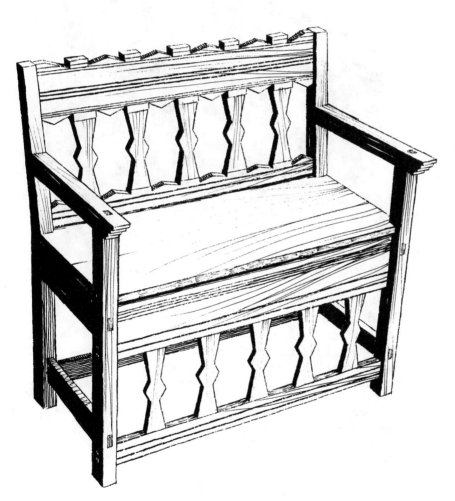

15-1 *Love seat.*

The original nineteenth-century bench, from the northern New Mexico area is now owned by the Museum of International Folk Art, part of the Museum of New Mexico. It is made of ponderosa pine, as were many large furniture items of the colonial period. The settee has been reproduced by E1 Rancho de las Golondrinas (see Fig. 15-2).

15-2 *A reproduction bench at El Rancho de las Golondrinas, Santa Fe.*

The decorative splats of the back and front are typical of the Southwestern style of the 1800s. Like other furniture of the Southwest, it is joined by mortise and tenons and has a solid wooden seat. As you can see in the photo, the seats were sometimes softened by draping handwoven blankets over them.

This is a wonderfully decorative and useful piece. It would be perfect for an entry hall or by the fireside. I feel that foam cushions covered with a woven fabric would be a practical addition.

You can use pine, poplar, teak, or mahogany for this project.

Part	Number Required	Size (inches)
A	1	¾ × 7 × 44*
B	1	¾ × 2½ × 44*
C	1	1 × 17 × 44 (can be made in two pieces)
D	1	¾ × 5½ × 44*
E	2	2 × 2½ × 44*
F	2	2 × 2 × 17*
G	2	2 × 2½ × 17*
H	1	¾ × 5½ × 44*
J	2	2 × 2 × 20*
K	2	2 × 2 × 28½*
L	2	2 × 5½ × 37
M	5	¾ × 2½ × 8
N	5	¾ × 2 × 8¼

*Allow 1 inch extra in both width and length for tenons.
Note: Measurements given are finished dimensions.

Miscellaneous:

Small round or square dowels for pinning through tenons.

1. Cut out basic pieces; allow extra for tenons in both length and width. See Figs. 15-3 through 15-10.
2. Sand.
3. Assemble two arm and leg sections. Cut mortises F, G, J, K, and L. Fit and trim tenons carefully until they all fit together well.
4. Assemble back section A, B, and M's. Assemble lower section D, E, and N's. Shape splats and glue them in place. See Figs. 15-8 and 15-9.
5. Cut decorative grooves and mortises in A, B, D, and E. See Fig. 15-11.
6. Cut and fit tenons on A, B, D, E, H, and back J so that they fit nicely into legs.
7. Trim off all tenons flush, and sand.
8. Pin through tenons.
9. Cut seat pieces to fit around legs.
10. Reassemble all parts. Glue and pin.
11. Sand and apply finish, unless you use mahogany or teak.

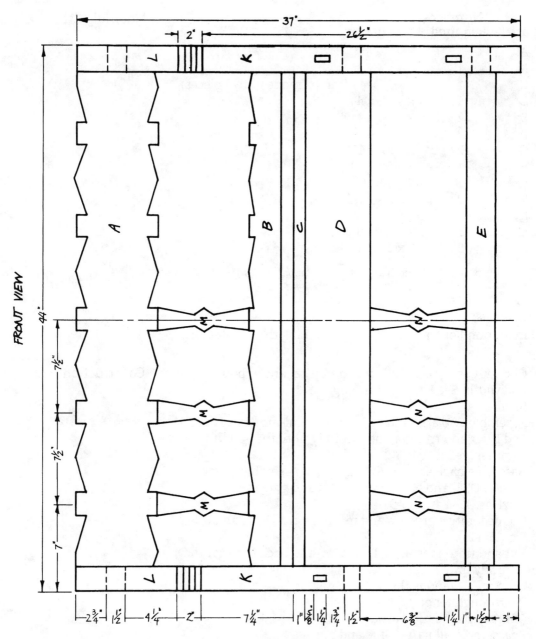

15-3 *Plan for the front assembly.*

102 Furniture

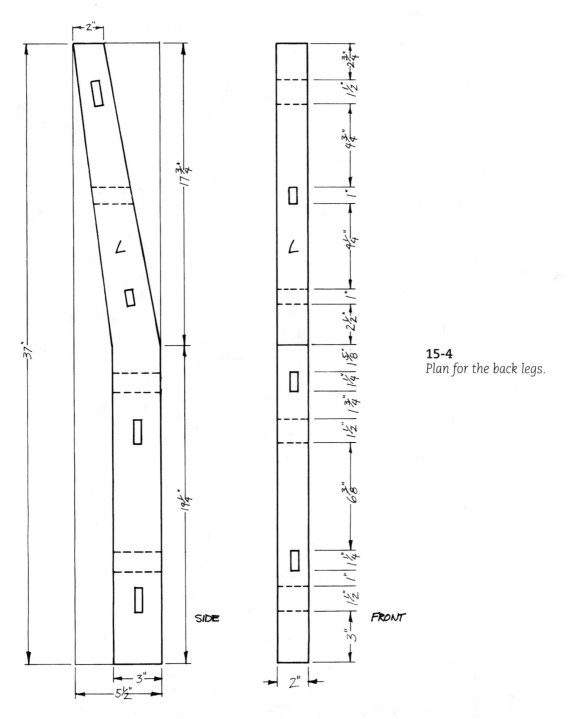

2"

17 3/4"

37"

L

19 1/4"

3"
5 1/2"

SIDE

2 3/4"
1/2"

4 3/4"

1"

4 1/4"

1"
2 1/2"
5/8"
1/4"
3/4"
1 1/2"

6 3/8"

1 1/2"
1"
1 1/4"

3"

2"

FRONT

15-4
Plan for the back legs.

Love seat with decorative splats   103

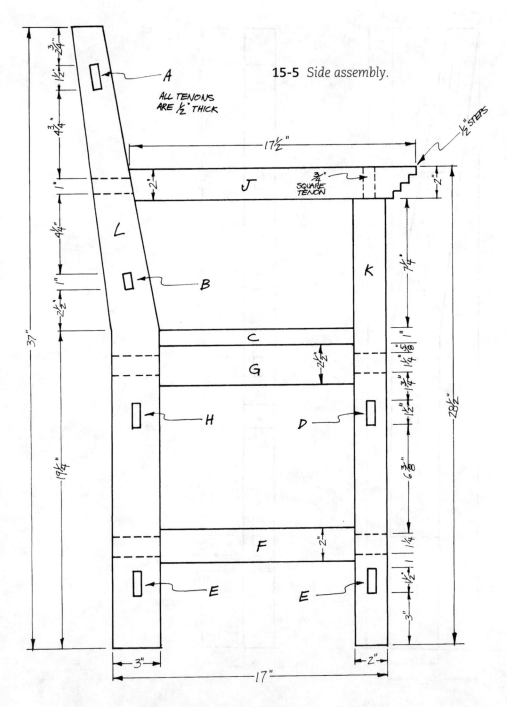

15-5 *Side assembly.*

A

ALL TENONS
ARE ½" THICK

½" STEPS

17½"

¾" SQUARE TENON

J

L

B

C

G

H

D

K

F

E

E

3"

2"

17"

104 Furniture

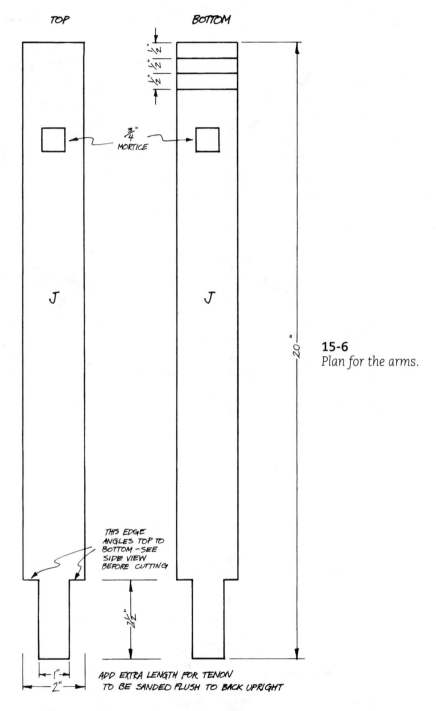

TOP

BOTTOM

$\frac{1}{2}$"

$\frac{1}{2}$"

$\frac{1}{2}$"

$\frac{3}{4}$"
MORTICE

J

J

20"

THIS EDGE
ANGLES TOP TO
BOTTOM – SEE
SIDE VIEW
BEFORE CUTTING

2$\frac{1}{2}$"

1"

2"

ADD EXTRA LENGTH FOR TENON
TO BE SANDED FLUSH TO BACK UPRIGHT

15-6
Plan for the arms.

Love seat with decorative splats 105

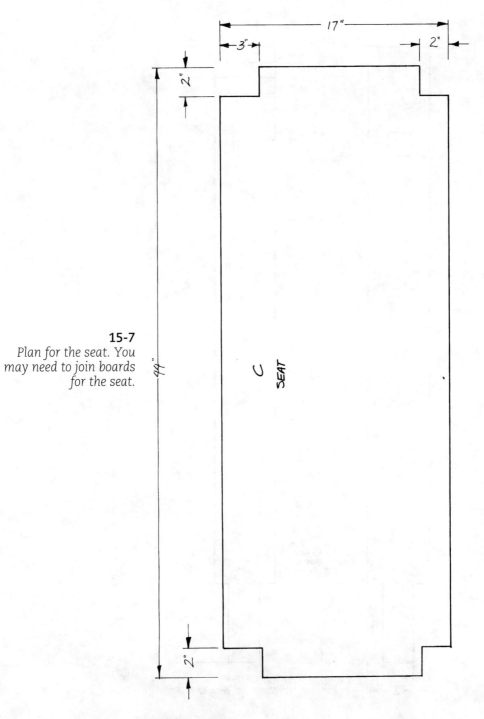

15-7
Plan for the seat. You may need to join boards for the seat.

C
SEAT

17"

3"

2"

2"

2"

44"

2"

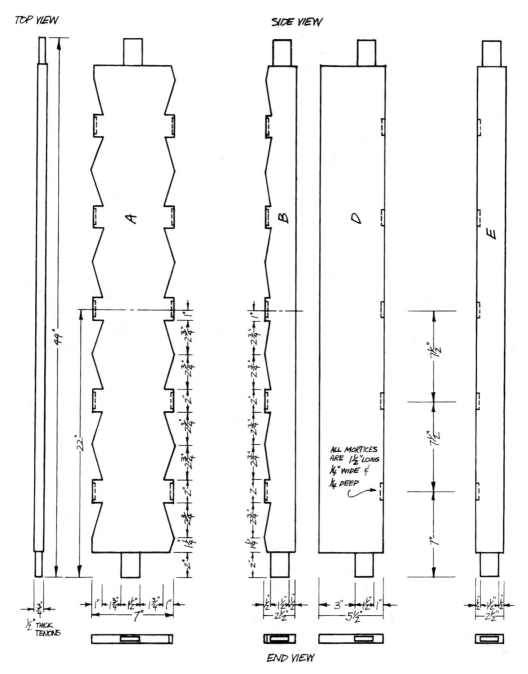

15-8 *Plan for rails A, B, D, and E.*

Love seat with decorative splats 107

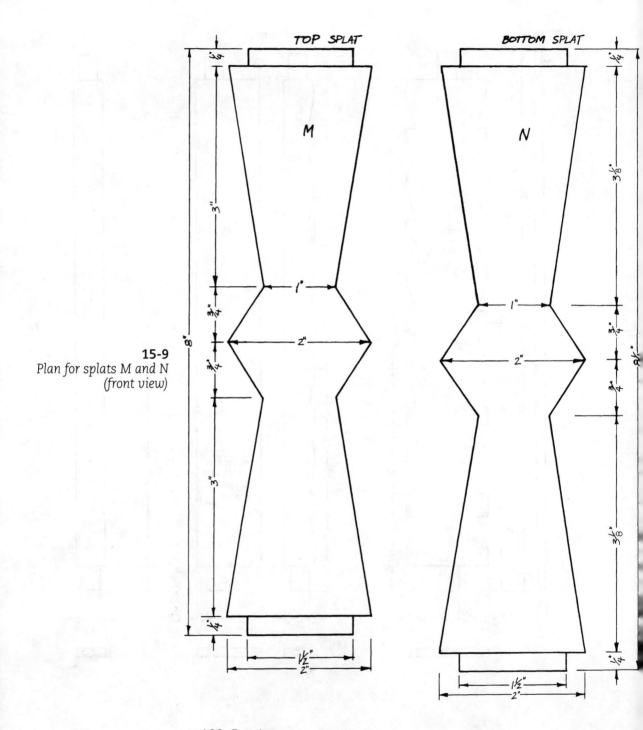

TOP SPLAT

BOTTOM SPLAT

M

N

1"

1"

2"

2"

15-9
*Plan for splats M and N
(front view)*

¼"

3"

¾"

¾"

3"

¼"

½"
2"

3⅛"

¾"

¾"

3⅛"

¼"

1½"
2"

8"

8½"

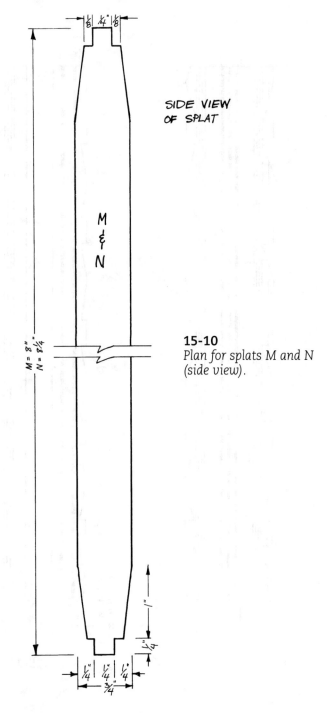

SIDE VIEW
OF SPLAT

M
&
N

15-10
*Plan for splats M and N
(side view).*

Love seat with decorative splats 109

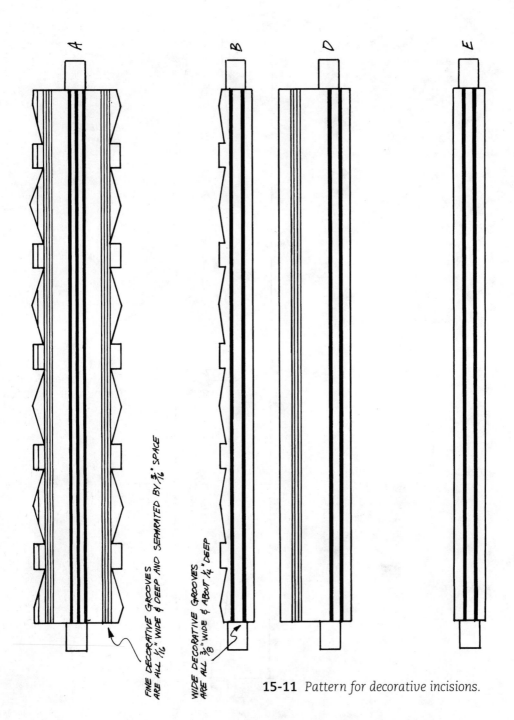

A

B

D

E

FINE DECORATIVE GROOVES ARE ALL $\frac{1}{16}$" WIDE & DEEP AND SEPARATED BY $\frac{3}{16}$" SPACE

WIDE DECORATIVE GROOVES ARE ALL $\frac{3}{8}$" WIDE & ABOUT $\frac{1}{4}$" DEEP

15-11 *Pattern for decorative incisions.*

110 Furniture

Display shelf and hanging rod

Painted bride's chest

*Padre's chair and
three-legged stool*

Bench

Miniature cart

Hanging shelf
with pegs

Tie-up shelf

Indian cradle

Sconce

Chandelier

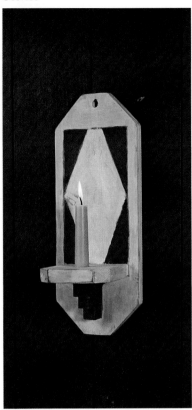

Occasional table with cheese tray

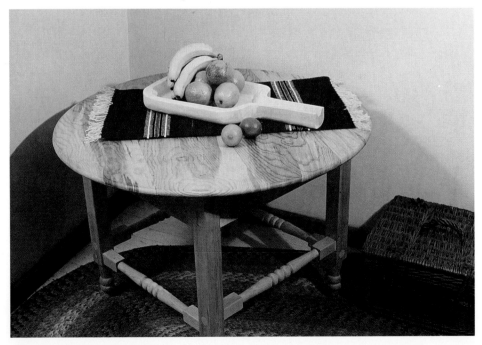

Armless chair (taburete)

W<small>HEN</small> I <small>FIRST</small> saw this little chair at El Rancho de las Golondrinas in Santa Fe, I immediately knew it should be included in this book. Its decorative splats, chip and incision decoration, and the pattern of its back and front runner (rails) are typical of the colonial style of the Southwest. The chair is small and appears to be a perfect lady's chair, so I was surprised to learn that it had originally been a priest's chair. The arms had been removed long ago, perhaps in order to allow a not-too-thin priest to sit on it.

The original of this chair was crafted during the first quarter of the nineteenth century in northern New Mexico. It includes all the features of a well-developed style of the Southwest (see Fig. 16-1). Made of unpainted ponderosa pine, it is joined by mortises and tenons. Its chipped and incised decoration reveals the blended geometric elements of Spanish and Latin motifs.

I hope you will have fun making this little chair. Even though the chair originally had arms, it seems perfectly proportioned as it is today.

Materials list

Part	Number Required	Size (inches)
A	1	¾ × 3 × 18*
B	1	¾ × 3 × 18*
C	2	¾ × 4 × 18*
D	2	¾ × 2 × 18*
E	2	¾ × 4 × 18*
F	2	¾ × 2 × 18*
G (legs)	2	2 × 4 × 36
H (legs)	2	2 × 2 × 16½
J (side brace)	2	¾ × 2 × 17*

K (side brace)	2	¾ × 2½ × 17*
L (splats)	2	¾ × 2½ × 10½ (for front only)
M (splats)	2	¾ × 2½ × 8½ (for front only)
S (seat)	1	1 × 17 × 18 (may be pieced together with biscuits or dowels)

*Allow 1 inch extra in both width and length for each tenon.
Note: Measurements given are finished dimensions.

Miscellaneous:
- $\frac{3}{16}$-inch dowels or pins for pinning pieces together; as needed
- Glue
- Chisels and mallet or rout bits to do incisions.

Construction tips

1. Cut out all blanks, according to Figs. 16-2 through 16-5. Make sure to allow extra length and width for tenons, which are to be trimmed flush after assembly. Seat may be pieced together at this point.
2. Cut mortises in all pieces.
3. Shape splats. Round corners and shape ends. See Fig. 16-6.
4. Chisel or rout decorative incisions on braces, as shown in Figs. 16-7 through 16-9.
5. Assemble sides, as in Fig 16-3. Glue and peg together.
6. Trim and fit splats into braces. Glue when a neat fit.
7. Assemble entire chair frame—sides and brace splat sections. When all pieces fit well, drill and pin through tenons as indicated.
8. Add seat, which can be pinned or screwed to frame. Be sure to sink and cover screws with plugs.
9. Cut off all tenons flush.
10. Sand smooth. Round all corners.
11. Apply sanding sealer and re-sand as often as needed to get a smooth finish.
12. Paint or varnish (matte finish), if desired.

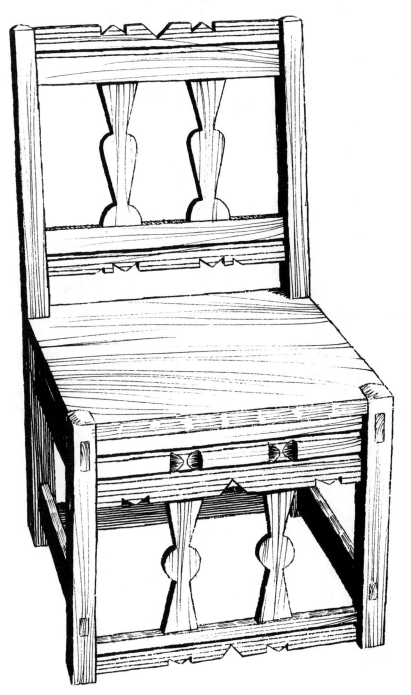

16-1
Armless chair.

Armless chair (taburete) 113

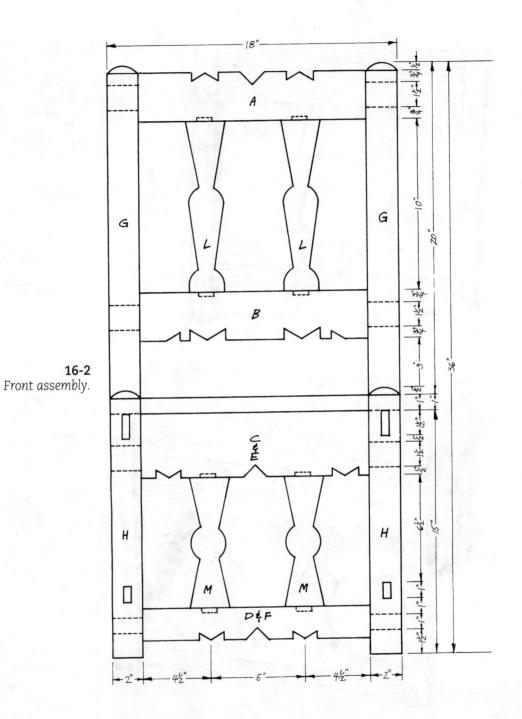

16-2
Front assembly.

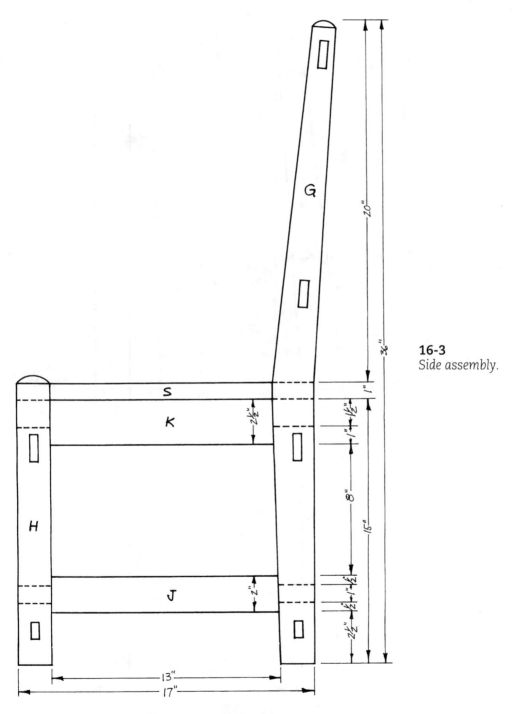

16-3
Side assembly.

Armless chair (taburete) 115

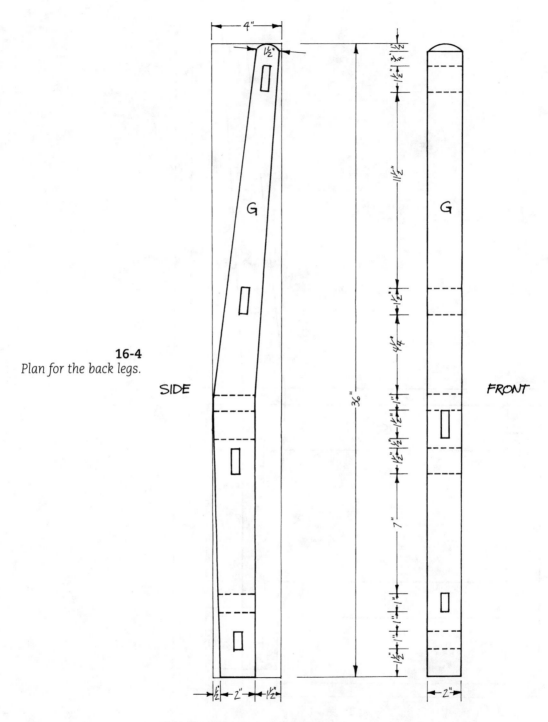

16-4
Plan for the back legs.

SIDE

FRONT

4"

1½"

G

G

36"

3"
½"

1½"

½"

4¼"

½"
1½"
½"

7"

1"
1"
½"

½" 2" 1½"

2"

16-5 *Plan for the seat.*

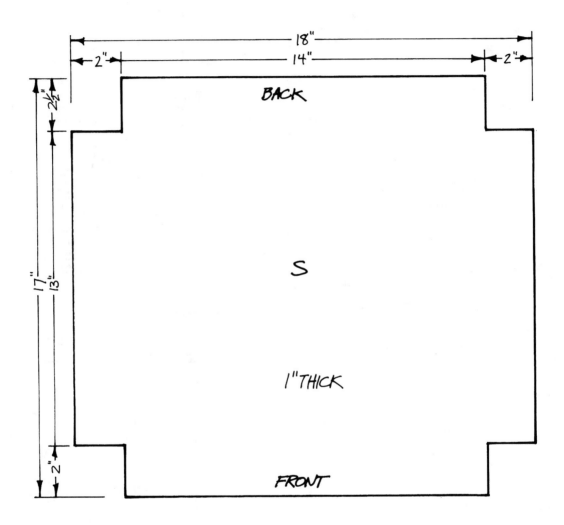

Armless chair (taburete) 117

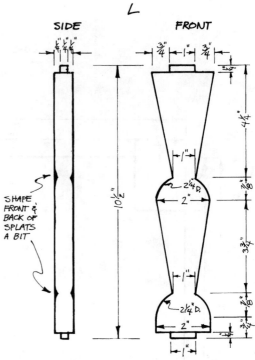

16-6 *Plan for the splats.*

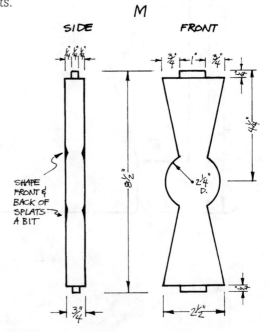

118 Furniture

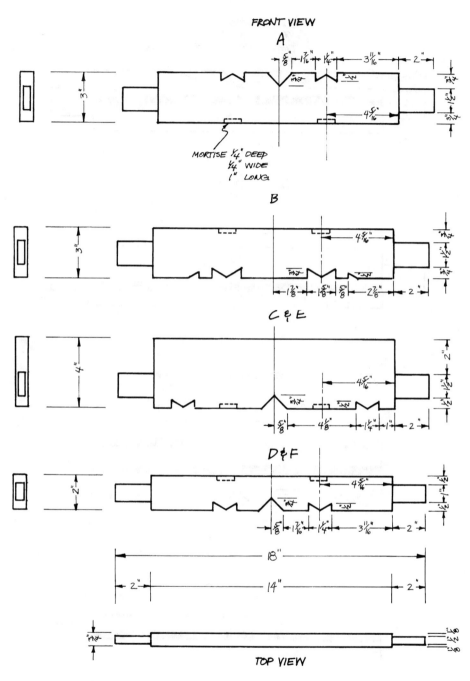

FRONT VIEW

A

MORTISE ¼" DEEP
¼" WIDE
1" LONG

B

C & E

D & F

TOP VIEW

16-7 Plan for the rails.

Armless chair (taburete) 119

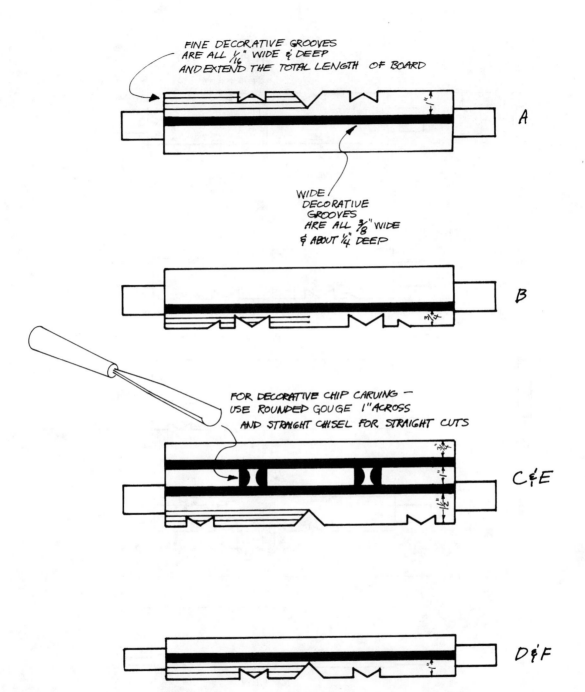

FINE DECORATIVE GROOVES
ARE ALL 1/16" WIDE & DEEP
AND EXTEND THE TOTAL LENGTH OF BOARD

1/4"

A

WIDE
DECORATIVE
GROOVES
ARE ALL 3/8" WIDE
& ABOUT 1/4" DEEP

3/4"

B

FOR DECORATIVE CHIP CARVING —
USE ROUNDED GOUGE 1" ACROSS
AND STRAIGHT CHISEL FOR STRAIGHT CUTS

3/4"
1"
1/2"

C & E

1/2"

D & F

16-8 *Patterns for incised decorations on rails.*

120 Furniture

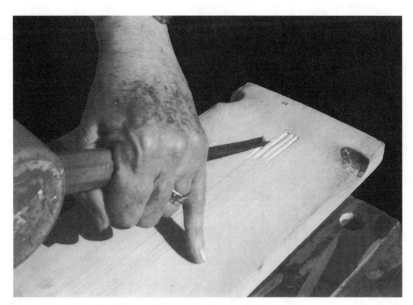

16-9 *Cutting incisions with a chisel.*

Armchair or padre's chair (sillón)

THIS ARMCHAIR is an attractive representation of the wooden armchairs generally reserved for use by priests or high officials. The simple, functional design features a wooden seat, fairly straight back with simple geometric cutout design, and gracefully curved armrests. See Figs. 17-1 and 17-2. A family usually possessed only one chair of this kind, and it was passed down through each generation. The few chairs still in existence are treasured by the families and museums that own them.

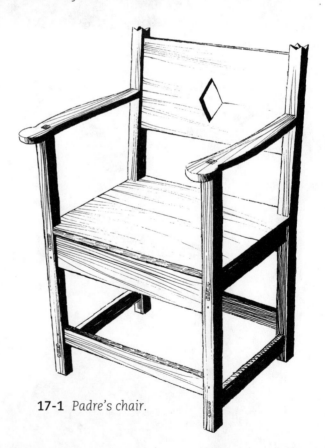

17-1 *Padre's chair.*

I patterned this project from a chair in the Hispanic section of a major Santa Fe museum. It is a reddish-brown color, so it might have been painted or stained at one time. The simple cutout of the back and the carved tops of the arm uprights are the only decorative elements. This chair has a simple dignity of its own. I feel that a homespun seat cushion would be a welcome and appropriate addition. Perhaps the early friars were provided with a cushion for long audiences unless they had ample padding of their own. Some *sillóns* of this type may have been originally covered with cloth or leather.

You can use ponderosa pine, teak, mahogany, cherry, or walnut for this project.

Materials list

Part	Number Required	Size (inches)
A (front legs)	2	1½ × 1½ × 28¾
B (back legs)	2	1½ × 3 × 36
C (arm)	2	¾ × 3 × 20½
D (lower braces)	2	¾ × 2 × 17
E (seat brace)	2	¾ × 2 × 17
F (lower braces)	2	¾ × 2 × 22
G (upper brace)	2	¾ × 4 × 22
H (upper backrest)	1	¾ × 6 × 22
I (lower backrest)	1	¾ × 4½ × 22
Seat	1	1 × 17¼ × 22 (can be pieced)

Note: Measurements given are finished dimensions. Allow an extra 1 inch in length for tenons. Trim after assembly.

Miscellaneous:

- Glue
- Wedges
- Sandpaper
- Sanding sealer

Construction tips

Note: See plans in Figs. 17-3 through 17-5 before proceeding.

1. Cut and join wood for seat, if necessary. Use biscuits or doweling for joining.
2. Cut H and I for backrest. Cut out diamond before joining pieces together. They can be joined with biscuits or dowels.
3. Cut arms and lay out. Shape and cut mortises.
4. Cut front legs. Leave tenons 1 inch long.
5. Cut mortises in front legs.
6. Lay on back legs and cut out.
7. Cut out mortises—follow plans.
8. Cut crowns on top of back legs. See Fig. 17-6.
9. Cut tenons on arms. Cut tenons little by little until they fit neatly into mortises. See Fig. 17-7.
10. Cut out braces.
11. Drill holes through tenons where shown in plans. Add dowel pins after assembly is completed. See Fig. 17-8.
12. Assemble chair in sections, as shown in Fig. 17-9.

13. Seat can be covered with fabric or leather, if desired, before fastening to frame.
14. When chair is assembled, add seat and pin it to frame. Figure 17-10 shows the chair prior to adding the seat.
15. Trim and sand. See Fig. 17-11.
16. Varnish, wax, or paint, as desired.

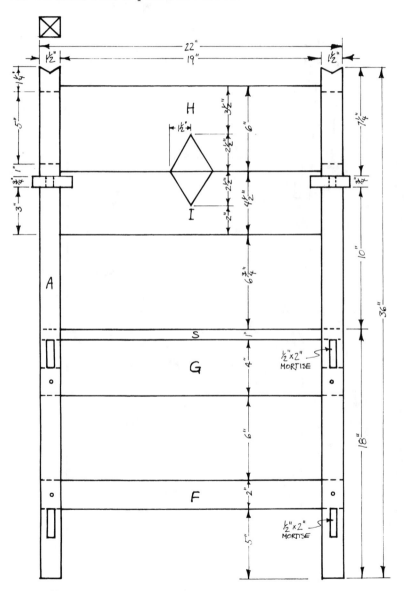

17-3
Front assembly.

Armchair or padre's chair (sillón) 125

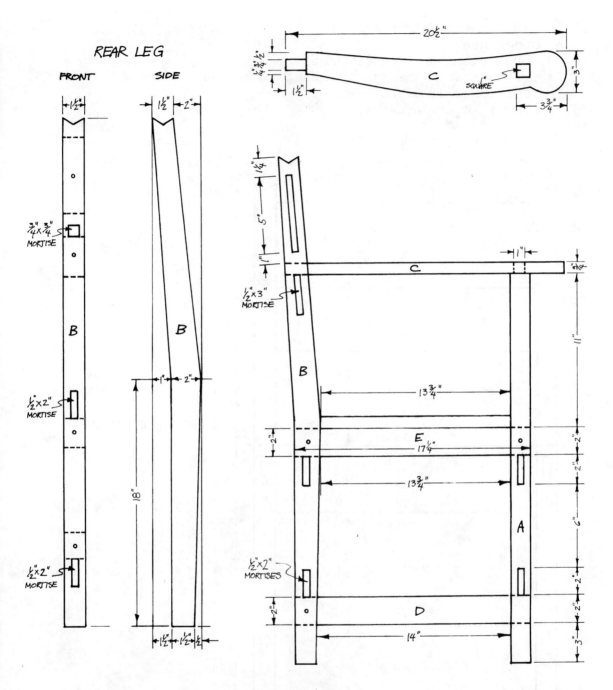

17-4 Plan for the sides and arms.

126 Furniture

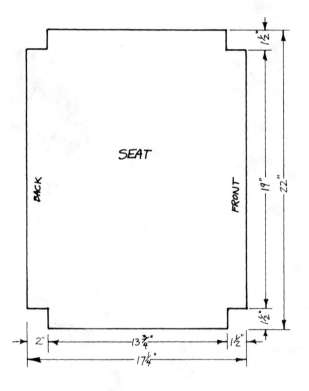

17-5 *Plan for the seat and scaled arm pattern.*
Enlarge squares to 1 inch.

SEAT

BACK

FRONT

1½"

19"

22"

1½"

2"

13¾"

1½"

17¼"

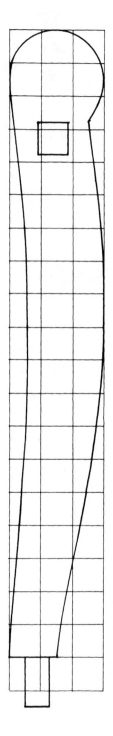

PATTERN FOR ARM

SQUARES ARE 1"

Armchair or padre's chair (sillón) 127

17-6
*Detail of the crown on top of
the back leg.*

17-7
*Detail of the arm with the
tenon wedged.*

128 Furniture

17-8
Detail of tenons and pinning.

17-9
Side assembly of the chair.

V.C. Chambers

Armchair or padre's chair (sillón)   129

17-10 Assembled chair before the tenons and pins are trimmed off and the seat added.

17-11 *Details of tenons and pegs in the legs, as shown in A and B, respectively.*

Armchair or padre's chair (sillón) 131

Tie-up shelf with painted edge (alazen)

I FIRST SAW this small shelf tied up to pegs and holding a variety of pottery containers. See Figs. 18-1 and 18-2. Smaller than many similar shelf pieces, it looked very useful on the narrow wall where it was hanging. I particularly liked the painted teal-blue and brick-red design on its edge. The remainder of the piece was unpainted, which is typical of the Southwestern style.

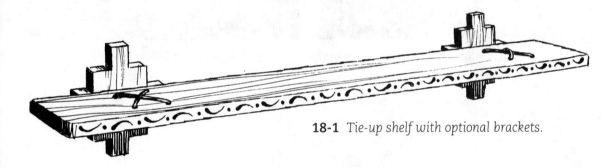

18-1 *Tie-up shelf with optional brackets.*

18-2
A reproduction shelf tied to brackets with leather thongs.

This would be a fun project for almost anyone to make, and it is also serviceable. I have added an alternative set of supports that makes it adaptable for use in a modern home, where you may not care to drive pegs into the wall.

You can use pine for this project.

Part	Number Required	Size (inches)	Notes
Shelf	1	¾ × 5½ × 36	(see Fig. 18-3)
Brackets (optional)	2	¾ × 5½ × 6	(see Fig. 18-4)

Note: Measurements given are finished dimensions.

Miscellaneous:
- 2¾-inch dowels, 6 inches long
- 2 long, thin leather thongs
- Paint, as desired—red, teal, or blue
- Glue, if desired

1. Cut out and drill all pieces. Sand well.
2. Mount dowels in brackets, and glue or wedge.
3. Paint decoration as desired. See pattern in Fig. 18-3.
4. Tie shelf to pegs in brackets.

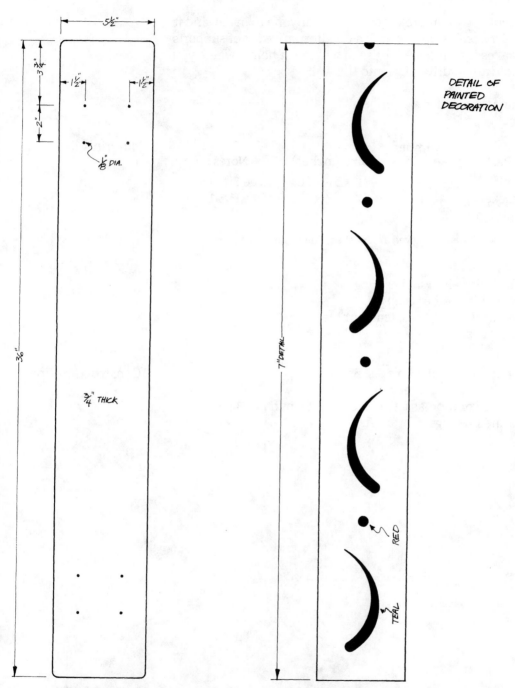

18-3 *Plan for a shelf and pattern for painted decoration.*

134 Furniture

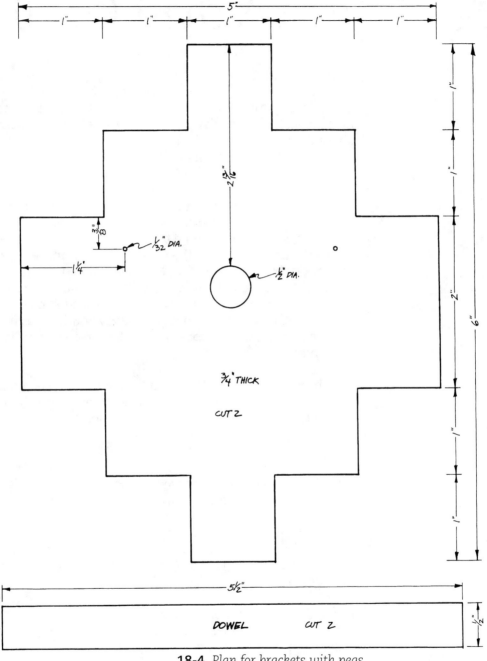

5"

1" 1" 1" 1" 1"

1"

1"

2 $\frac{3}{16}$"

6"

2"

$\frac{3}{8}$"

$\frac{1}{32}$" DIA.

$\frac{1}{2}$" DIA.

1 $\frac{1}{4}$"

$\frac{3}{4}$" THICK

CUT 2

1"

1"

5 $\frac{1}{2}$"

DOWEL   CUT 2

$\frac{1}{2}$"

18-4 *Plan for brackets with pegs.*

Tie-up shelf with painted edge (alazen) 135

Bride's chest (arca)

SMALL WOODEN chests of this type were treasured heirlooms in the homes of early Hispanic colonists. Often called bride's chests, they perhaps held a wife's dowry when she went to her new home. In the Spanish tradition, the chests were raised above the floor on trunk stands (racks) to prevent the dampness of earthen floors from damaging the bottoms of the chests.

The chests were often painted or carved in bold geometric or stylized pictorial scenes. Some chests were elaborately carved on the sides, but never on the tops. Chests were sometimes used as seats, and carving the tops would have made them uncomfortable. Both the carved and the painted chests usually had locks with decorative plates, which were an important part of the total design. However embellished, a bride's chest served as a colorful decorative focus for the early Southwestern home with its smooth, white adobe walls and sparse, unpainted furnishings.

The chest shown in Figs. 19-1 and 19-2 has a bold geometric painting accentuated by a heart-shaped wrought iron lock. It is an outstanding example of Spanish tradition blending with native Indian motifs and local materials.

The pattern for this project includes the traditional heavy dovetailing, which is also pegged. See Fig. 19-3. The top is attached with small inside hinges. I include a plan for the painting and for making the iron heart-shaped plate for a lock. You can mount a contemporary lock behind the heart or omit the lock altogether. If you do not make a metal heart plate for the front, paint one instead. The heart is an integral part of the front design.

The bride's chest was often fitted with a bank of small drawers against one side of the interiors, as shown in Fig. 19-4. I did not include the drawers in my plans.

19-1
Bride's chest.

19-2
A reproduction bride's chest.

Bride's chest (arca) 137

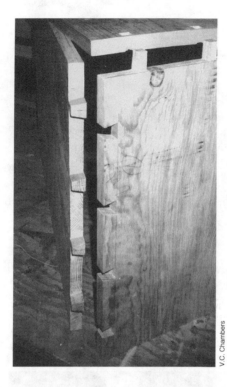

19-3
View showing dovetails in the side and square pegs in the top of the chest. Dowels may be used instead of pegs, if desired.

V.C. Chambers

Most old bride's chests have long histories passed down through generations, but many families have long forgotten the exact age of their chests.

Use pine or another even, fine-grained wood of your choice.

Materials list

Part	Number Required	Size (inches)	Notes
Top (A)	1	$^3/_4 \times 16 \times 29$	(allow an extra inch)
Flanges or ears (B)	2	$^3/_4 \times 3 \times 16$	
Front & back (C)	2	$^3/_4 \times 16 \times 27\frac{1}{2}$	(allow an extra inch)
Ends (E)	2	$^3/_4 \times 16 \times 16$	
Bottom (D)	1	$^3/_4 \times 16 \times 27\frac{1}{2}$	

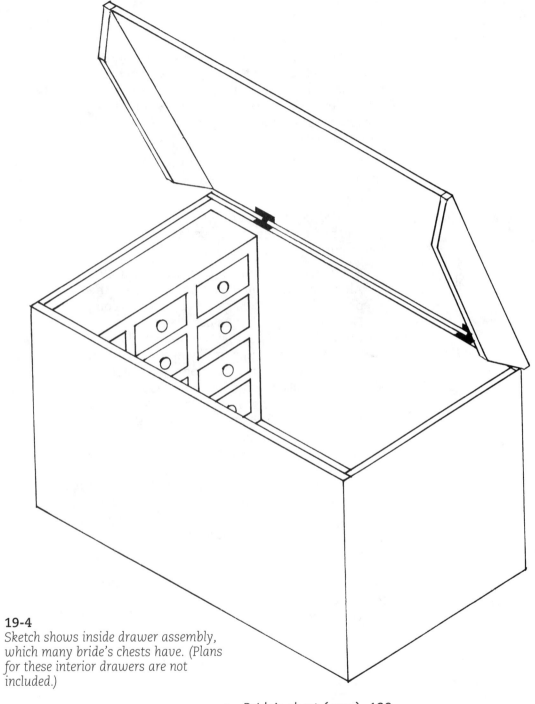

19-4
*Sketch shows inside drawer assembly,
which many bride's chests have. (Plans
for these interior drawers are not
included.)*

Miscellaneous:

- glue
- ⅜-inch doweling or square pegs to fasten bottom to sides (if desired, use screws and cover with plugs)
- 2 inside iron hinges for fastening top of chest
- 1 iron heart lock and hinge for outside (if you cannot get a heart to fit the pattern, incorporate the heart as part of the painted design and put a plain wrought iron fastening fixture on the front of the chest).

Note: Measurements given are finished dimensions. Allow an extra 1 inch on each end where there are tenons.

Construction tips   If you need to join wood to get the desired width, use dowels or biscuits and glue. Leave clamped for a day, then sand well before cutting out the pattern.

1. Cut blanks for all major pieces. See Figs. 19-5 and 19-6. Allow an extra 1 inch on each side where there are tenons or dovetails. Cut flush after assembly is complete.
2. Drill mortises in flanges between B.
3. Cut tenons in top A to fit mortises in flanges B (Fig. 19-7). Trim and fit carefully until you get a tight fit. Glue before the final fit. Wedge tenons only if necessary.
4. Cut dovetails in front, back, and ends.
5. Fine fit until you get a tight match. Glue, if desired.
6. Peg C to Bs with square pegs or dowels.
7. Fasten bottom D to box with glue and dowels set at opposing angles or with pegs, as shown in Fig. 19-8.
8. Sand all parts of chest, and round edges slightly.
9. Finish wood as desired. If painting, follow patterns in Figs. 19-9 and 19-10. Paint all pieces white with thin paint. Rub them down to give a worn look.
10. Trace outline of pattern on white base.
11. Paint pattern with as loose a style as possible.
12. Sand and rub to give a well-used look.
13. Finish with a matte finish protective coat.
14. Fasten on hinges and decorative heart latch. (See Figs. 19-11 and 19-12). If you cannot get metal cut in a heart shape, include the heart shape with the painted design.

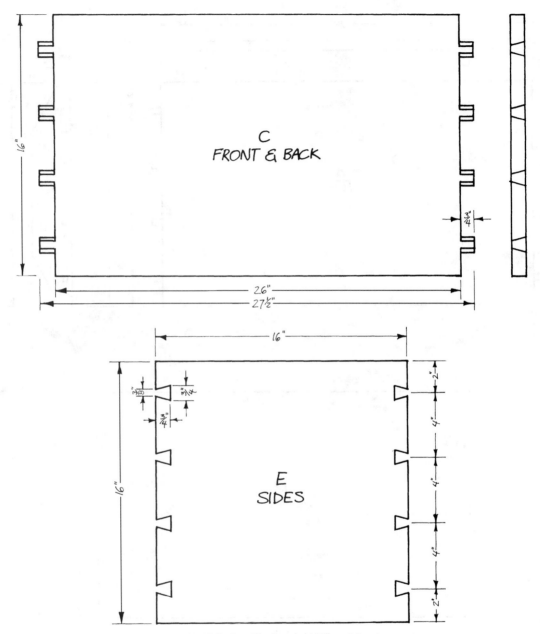

19-5 *Plan for the front, side, and back.*

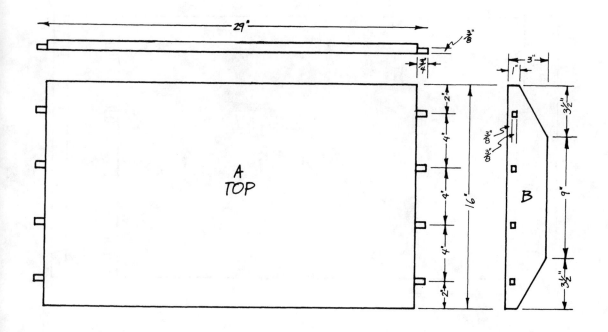

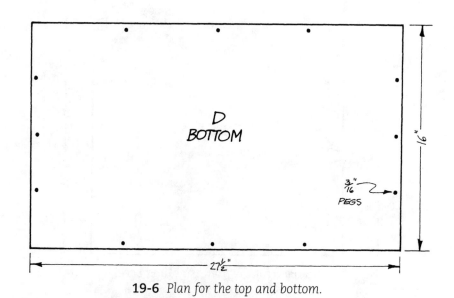

19-6 *Plan for the top and bottom.*

142 Furniture

19-7
Detail of flanges on the top that shows square tenons.

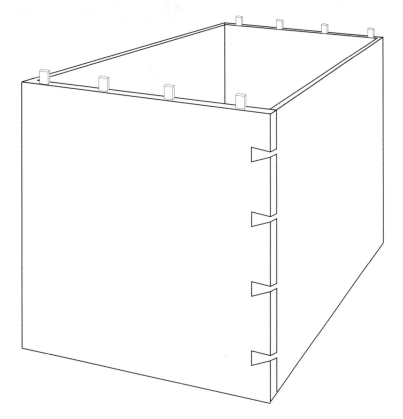

19-8
Illustration shows square pegs that join the bottom to the chest.

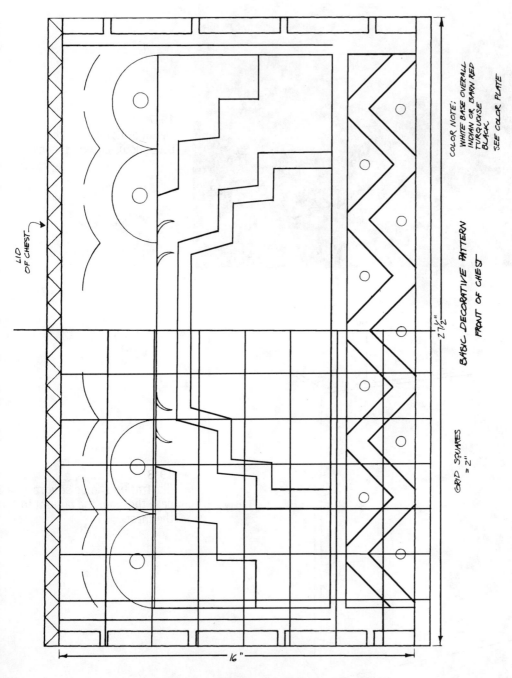

COLOR NOTE:
WHITE BASE OVERALL
INDIAN OR BARN RED
TURQUOISE
BLACK

SEE COLOR PLATE

BASIC DECORATIVE PATTERN
FRONT OF CHEST

LID OF CHEST

GRID SQUARES = 2"

2½"

16"

19-9 *Pattern for painted design on the front.*

144 Furniture

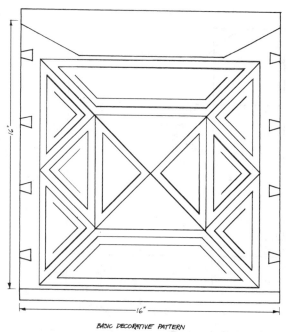

19-10
Pattern for painted design on the sides.

BASIC DECORATIVE PATTERN
SIDE OF CHEST

16"

COLOR NOTE:
WHITE BASE OVERALL
INDIAN OR BARN RED
TURQUOISE
BLACK
SEE COLOR PLATE

19-11
Detail shows hinges inside the chest.

Bride's chest (arca) 145

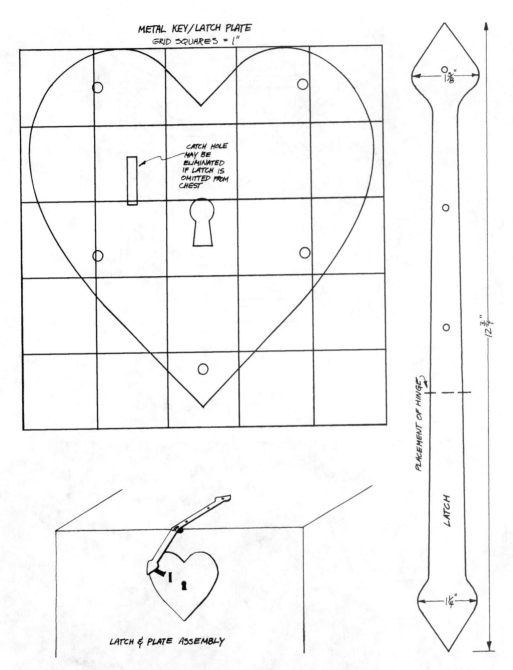

METAL KEY/LATCH PLATE
GRID SQUARES = 1"

CATCH HOLE MAY BE ELIMINATED IF LATCH IS OMITTED FROM CHEST

$\frac{3}{8}$"

12 $\frac{3}{4}$"

PLACEMENT OF HINGE

LATCH

1 $\frac{1}{4}$"

LATCH & PLATE ASSEMBLY

19-12 Pattern for making the metal heart latch. If you cannot find get a latch that works with this pattern, paint on the heart as a decoration only.

146 Furniture

Occasional table (mesa)

TABLES WERE a luxury in the homes of the early colonists. They were not used for dining, but rather as writing desks or for holding special items, such as record books or Bibles. Tables were made one at a time and by different craftsmen, so each one is unique. Most tabletops were rectangular or square and rested on square-leg assemblies. Typically, the tables have wide aprons and quite sturdy legs and stringers.

The little table shown in Figs. 20-1 and 20-2 has a round top, which is supported by a square-leg assembly. Although simple in design compared with many other tables of the period, its elegant square legs complement the round top.

20-1 *Occasional table.*

20-2
A reproduction table.

If you want to make only one piece in the Southwestern style for your own home, this table would be a good choice.

Following the pattern given here, you can make a perfect end table or a high coffee table. If you want to make it suitable for dining, add 5 or 6 inches to the legs to make it taller. Use pine, teak, or mahogany for this project.

Materials list

Part	Number Required	Size (inches)	Notes
Top	1	¾ × 36 × 36	Make by doweling
A	2	inches round	or biscuiting together
B	2	¾ × 5 × 23*	several boards
Leg (C)	4	¾ × 5 × 23*	(see Fig. 20-3).
Stretchers (D)	4	2 × 2 × 24**	
		1½ × 1½ × 23*	

*Allow 1 inch extra in length for tenons.
**Allow 1 inch extra in length for tenons and ½ inch extra for trimming.
 Note: Measurements are given as finished dimensions.

20-3
How wood is joined for the tabletop.

V.C. Chambers

Miscellaneous:
- Dowels or pegs for pinning through tenons
- Wedges
- Glue, if desired.

Construction tips

1. Join wood for tabletop. Glue and clamp for 24 hours; then cut out. See Fig. 20-4.
2. Round the edge of tabletop.
3. Cut and trim legs and stretchers according to patterns in Figs. 20-5 through 20-7.
4. Turn legs and stretchers on a lathe.
5. Cut mortises in legs. Note: Mortises for stretchers will be round.
6. Shape tenons. Note: Tenons at ends of stretchers are round, and tops of legs are round.
7. Cut out sides. See Fig. 20-8.
8. Join one side, two legs, and one stretcher together, as in Fig. 20-8.
9. Join sections together, as in step 8, to form complete base assembly.
10. Turn base assembly upside down on tabletop. Mark location of leg tenons on tabletop in order to cut for mortise.
11. Cut round mortises in tabletop.

12. Join tabletop to base.
13. Wedge tenons and cut off flush. See Fig. 20-9.
14. Sand.
15. Wax, varnish, or paint, as desired. Figures 20-10 and 20-11 show details of the completed table.

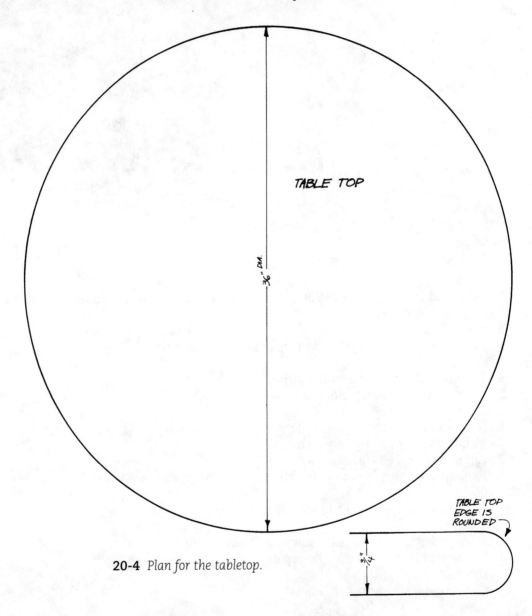

TABLE TOP

36" DIA.

TABLE TOP EDGE IS ROUNDED

3/4"

20-4 *Plan for the tabletop.*

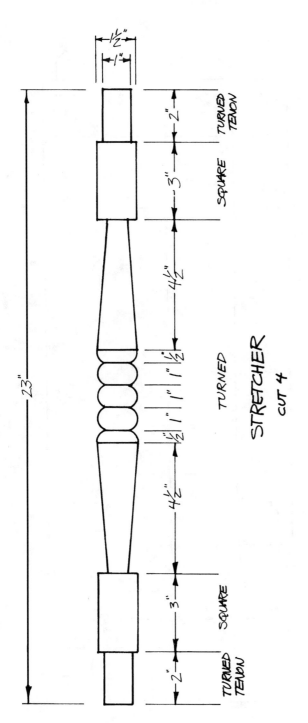

1½"
1"

23"

TURNED TENON
2"

SQUARE
3"

TURNED
4½"

1½" 1" 1" ½"
½" 1" 1" ½"

4½"

SQUARE
3"

TURNED TENON
2"

STRETCHER
CUT 4

20-5
Plan for the stretchers.

Occasional table (mesa) 151

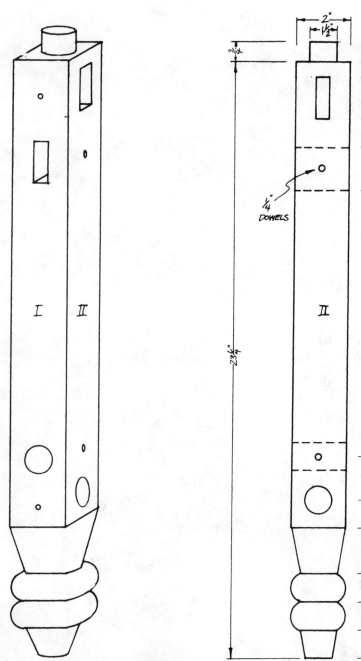
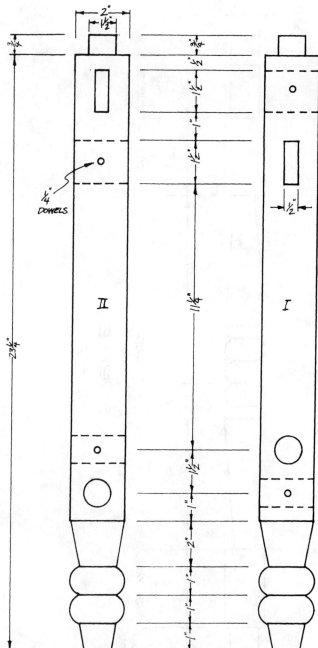

20-6 *Plan for the legs.*

PATTERN FOR
TURNED SECTION OF STRETCHER

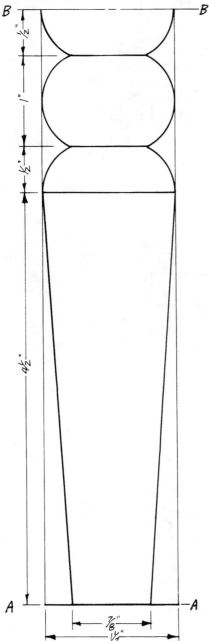

B   B

½"

1"

½"

4½"

A   A

⅞"

1½"

PATTERN FOR
LOWER PART OF LEGS

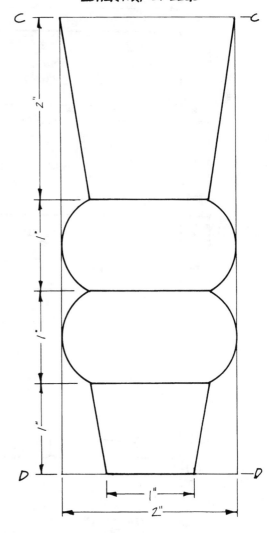

C   C

2"

1"

1"

1"

D   D

1"

2"

20-7 Plan for the turned portion of the legs and
stretchers. If you do not have a lathe, these parts
can be carved.

Occasional table (mesa) 153

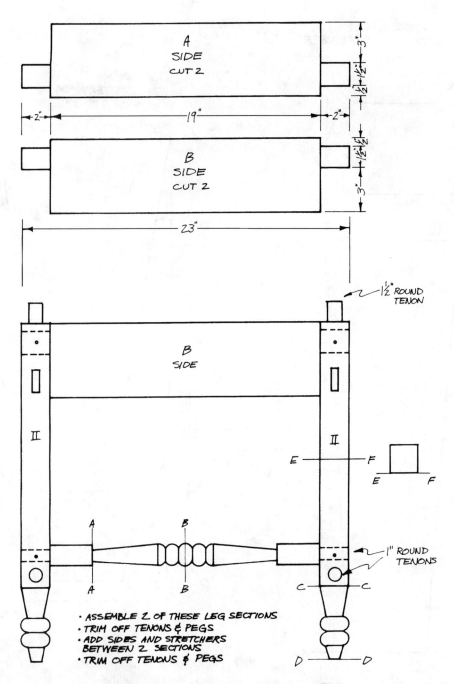

20-8 *Plan for the sides and base assembly.*

154 Furniture

20-9
Detail of top of the legs after tenons and pins are trimmed.

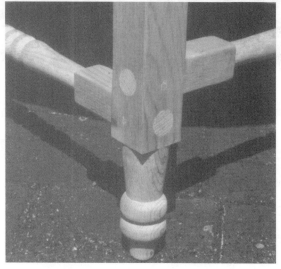

20-10
Detail of mortises in a leg when finished and pegged.

Occasional table (mesa) 155

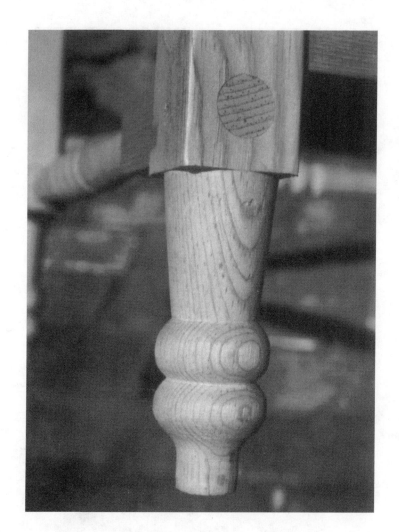

20-11
Bottom of a finished leg.